DESIGNERS HERE AND THERE

MARTHA ANGUS

SAN FRANCISCO, CALIFORNIA & ST. HELENA, CALIFORNIA

CONTENTS

ACKNOWLEDGMENTS

I am most grateful to all the designers who participated in the book for opening their homes—and oftentimes their hearts—to me, and for providing the beautiful photographs that allow us a behind-the-scenes glimpse into their lives. I am honored to have worked with these gifted artists and to have become acquainted with each of them on a more personal level.

I would also like to thank Stacee Lawrence, my editor at the Monacelli Press, whose enthusiasm never wavered and was a joy to work with; Andrea Monfried, for believing in the project and for bringing me on board; Elizabeth White, for her commitment to reproducing the designers' work so accurately; Sara Stemen, for her great design; the photographers and magazines who contributed and allowed our use of their lovely images; friends and colleagues whose unflagging support kept me going through thick and thin, especially Rhonda Cole, Jerry Hasson, Daniel Kennedy, and Colette Landi Sipperly; and my sisters Nichole and Alexandra, who are always there for me with words of wisdom, encouragement, and their wonderful senses of humor.

Library of Congress Cataloging-in-Publication Data
Keith, Michele.
Designers here and there / by Michele Keith.—1st ed.
p. cm.
Includes bibliographical references and index.
ISBN 978-1-58093-246-2 (hardcover : alk. paper)
1. Interior decorators—Homes and haunts—United States.
2. Interior decoration—United States. I. Title.
NK2115.3.I57K45 2010
747—dc22   2009042910

Printed in China
www.monacellipress.com

10 9 8 7 6 5 4 3 2
First edition

Designed by Sara E. Stemen

DESIGNERS HERE AND THERE

INSIDE THE CITY AND COUNTRY HOMES OF AMERICA'S TOP DECORATORS

MICHELE KEITH

THE MONACELLI PRESS

Contemporary art looms large in Martha Angus's life and is at the heart of her business. A painter since childhood, she turned to interior design at the suggestion of her parents, who were concerned the starving-artist syndrome might befall her. Known for her unexpected ways of mixing colors and furniture styles, Angus also enjoys an enviable reputation for guiding art collectors with their acquisitions. Her home atop San Francisco's Nob Hill leaps between the seventeenth century and the twenty-first with colors both intense and mellow, while her weekend retreat in St. Helena is crisp, but easy with antiques and hues picked up from the garden. Not surprisingly, art figures prominently in both.

"Art is everywhere, even on the floor."

This Art Deco–era apartment featuring spectacular views of San Francisco Bay and the Golden Gate Bridge has been home to Angus since 2003. For a long time her style tended to the traditional, verging on formal, with few shots of color. The idea of freshening the 1,500-square-foot space took hold gradually. "My son Malcolm had been begging me to go modern for years," she says, "so I began little by little." First came the mirrored, 1970s coffee tables and some "inexpensive, darned good-looking" accent pieces in the living room. "I finished up with pizzazz," she says, noting the Roy Lichtenstein silkscreen and rug.

The rest of the apartment is muted, although as Angus says, "It all hangs together with blue accents and pop art in nearly every room." A stack of Andy Warhol's *Brillo Boxes* and a David Salle aquatint can be found in the bedroom, for example, and in her son's room, there is a fiberglass pastil chair by Eero Aarnio. She propels the predominantly eighteenth- and nineteenth-century furniture into the present by decorating rooms sparsely to draw attention to individual pieces, as with the Gustavian settee—whose sleek lines belie its 200 years—and the lone Directoire *chauffeuse*—stark against the hallway's creamy walls, turning them into veritable works of art.

Objects of every era and price point are welcomed. Angus advises, "If it works, use it." In the bedroom, an ordinary white plate placed over the top of a Portuguese water urn from the 1700s turns it into a side table. In the bathroom, a neoclassical Italian parcel-gilt chair—perhaps the finest piece of furniture she owns—pulls up to a Parsons-style makeup table with a silvery, carlike finish, from a catalog. As for the portrait? There is no artist's signature, but it inspires her to put some extra effort into dressing for the day.

Angus rarely entertains large crowds in the city, but when she does, the table beneath the cheeky painting of Jayne Mansfield in the dining area expands to seat eight. Like many of the furnishings, the table comes with a story. "I had to fight off another designer to get it," she says, laughing. Both saw it at their favorite Paris flea market as the dealer was leaving for the evening. "I returned the next day at the crack of dawn," she gleefully recounts, "and got it before she even arrived!"

Angus's commute home is a short but steep three-block walk from her office. The apartment welcomes her back every day with its pumped up color that is nevertheless quietly serene.

"Weekends couldn't get much better. This place is for unwinding, not working."

St. Helena reminds me of Southampton, Long Island, where I summered for twenty years," reminisces East Coast native Angus. She had been looking for a weekend house in this Napa Valley town to recapture that spirit when she came across an Internet ad for property that was barren save for a dilapidated chicken coop. Later that same day, she was gazing at magnificent old oaks and views of the mountains. She was smitten. The coop quickly came down and a simplified neo-Palladian villa slowly went up.

The interior expresses what Angus loves most, "a neutral envelope with accents dictated by colorful art." Warhol's yellows, oranges, and violets replay in the master bedroom's 1940s Aubusson tapestry throw. In the kitchen, an Ellsworth Kelly lithograph underscores the blue lavastone island. And the colors here reflect what she sees outside the windows too: the leafy tones in a Mark Mentzer painting inspired the ground floor's palette. Angus erases any thoughts of taking her art too seriously, however, by popping quirky items into unexpected places. Some, like a red plastic rocket poised to blast off from the top of the stairs, are just plain fun. Others, like the library's 150-year-old "screaming fuchsia" folding chair by George Hunzinger, carry impeccable pedigrees. "I buy things I like and worry about where to put them when I get home," she says.

"No wet bathing suits in the living room" is one of her few rules, but it's still the country; kids run in and out and sneakers track in dirt, so why take a chance? A Louis XVI settee is covered in outdoor chenille; the curvy eighteenth-century Directoire bench is dressed in ribbed cotton; and facing the white coffee table—actually an upended sculpture— are club chairs upholstered in Jim Thompson Thai cotton blend. The bronze-legged fireside stools fit right in with rugged cowhide cushions. Here Angus's favorite method of relaxation, stretching out on the sofa and reading about history's most accomplished women, is interrupted only by neighbors stopping in after touring nearby vineyards.

ANDREW FISHER & JEFFRY WEISMAN

SAN FRANCISCO, CALIFORNIA & HEALDSBURG, CALIFORNIA

Andrew Fisher and Jeffry Weisman are polar opposites. Fisher is driven by unbridled imagination, Weisman by practical restraint. This dichotomy lends a unique power to their design approach, and each of their homes exhibits its sophisticated results. Their San Francisco apartment, designed with a focus on entertaining clients and friends, is pure glamour. Their house in Sonoma County's wine country is geared toward casual, daytime living. While an escape, they also love working there: Fisher crafts ornamental wonders in the studio as Weisman dots the i's and crosses the t's on the firm's myriad projects in the library. Two men, two strengths, one successful partnership.

"Dim the lights, turn on the music, you have a party."

Twinkling stars and sparkling city lights outside Fisher and Weisman's Nob Hill apartment vie for attention with the host of shimmering adornments on its interior. Ensconced in a 1926 building that conjures Gatsby-era images, their home gleams with candlelight, lacquered wood, and furnishings ranging from contemporary tables with delicate bases that evoke gilded twigs to Louis XVI chairs that look as at home here surrounded by walls of antiqued mirrors as they would have at Versailles. "We're never here during the day or on weekends," says Fisher. "The space is really for entertaining three or four nights a week." Played out against deep chocolate brown accented with coral, the quiet glamour is unequivocally seductive.

"Let's be gracious," laughs Weisman as he begins describing the apartment's original condition. "It wasn't to our taste." It proved quite a feat to rework the layout to suit their needs. They constructed a dining room from the entry, enlarged the master bedroom, and created a kitchen on par with Fisher's four-star cooking by combining the small original with the butler's pantry. It now contains a complete range of professional equipment; the pantry houses the apartment's audio system, bar, wine refrigerator, second sink and dishwasher, plus ample storage for china and glassware.

The living room best encapsulates the two men's design theory. As Weisman explains, "You can have just so much over-the-top stuff. Then the eye needs a break." While there are attention-getting pieces—an eighteenth-century Portuguese mirror, brass-and-mahogany chairs upholstered with woven peacock feathers, towering candlesticks that reach from the floor to the mantlepiece—they are outnumbered by the areas of calm, most notably the bare hardwood floors and straight-edged tables and chests. This technique, as the designer points out, allows the eye to fully appreciate each object's beauty.

Fisher's art also provides visual pauses. "You can't live with an artist and not expect to have lots of his work on the walls," his partner jokes. Above the sofa is one of his most creative pieces: a quilt of painted and gilded coffee filters cut apart, then sewn back together with silk thread. Another, a shell-encrusted chandelier, is in the dining room. It's a showstopper against the pewter-leaf ceiling and handblown, glass panels that compensate for the room's lack of windows. The mother-of-pearl-topped table adds another layer of interest, but as elsewhere, the designers stop just short of crossing the line into pageantry.

In the bedroom, comfort beckons at evening's end: flannel-covered walls, watercolors by Russian set designer Eugene Berman—one lavishly framed to anchor the group—and a stately canopy bed draped with yard upon yard of sumptuous fabric. No drama here, simply muted elegance before the next hectic day.

"The exterior is subtly classical . . . the interior lighthearted glamour."

J ust walking through the house makes me smile," says Weisman, "It's alive with memories of the past fifteen years," continues Fisher. They claim that mixing together their hoard of belongings—inherited pieces and furnishings picked up while exploring far-flung countries—was as much fun as building the house. Easy, too. They only needed to purchase a few items as glue to bind the design together. But as Fisher admits, "There were a few wild cards in the bunch. Some pieces made it, others didn't." Weisman feels there is an assumption that country houses must be white and airy, but that's not them. Instead, the house's style is, as they affectionately refer to it, "Mussolini Meets Doris Duke," capricious surprises within a pared-down architectural frame.

Flooded with sunlight, the 600-square-foot living room sizzles with originality. The pair designed the extra-wide sofas with a curve so those sitting at the ends can see each other. "We found antique silk saris in India with worn spots and a few holes, but also glistening with 24-karat-gold thread," smiles Fisher. "The dealer thought we were crazy to buy them, but when we got them home, we cut out the bad parts and sewed the pieces together to make fanciful uphol-stery for the slipper chairs." The patterns and tex-tures of carpets lugged back from Morocco contrast with the reclaimed-oak flooring. And because nights can be noisy—workers are often out tending the sur-rounding vineyards—the gossamer linen draperies are double-lined with worsted wool.

The ample kitchen represents the first where the two have had enough space for a full-sized table, perfect for spreading out maps of their vineyard and olive orchard to chart new plantings or to plot refine-ments to the rose garden. Antique Japanese painted panels that once decorated the ceiling of a temple enrich the otherwise simple space, and faux bois doors with camel-bone knobs often surprise guests who think they are bona fide wood. In their inimitable fashion, the designers used these beguiling touches to transition the pragmatic room into the whimsical world of the rest of the house.

The men have a constant stream of weekend visitors who usually stay in the pool-house-cum-guest-cottage. But when that is full, their company is all too happy to hear, "Go outside and turn left," for a 400-square-foot tree house awaits. Straddling two soaring firs, as exquisitely appointed as the main house with a four-poster bed of their own design, touches of faux tortoise and bird's eye maple, gold leaf, gold-glazed linen draperies, and furniture sheathed in layers of shells—it is a fairy tale come true.

STEPHEN SHUBEL

SAN FRANCISCO, CALIFORNIA & SAUSALITO, CALIFORNIA

"My experience in France colors every design decision I make," says Stephen Shubel, former resident of a chic Paris apartment and current owner of a vacation house in the Loire Valley. Now he lives primarily in San Francisco where a spacious loft serves as both home and office and brings to mind a sophisticated atelier with its crossover mix of classical antiques and contemporary furnishings. Long weekends find him across the bay in a renovated, 1907 fishing cottage lodged into a Sausalito hillside. Crisply black and white, it is American casual . . . with a healthy dose of Parisian elegance.

"I don't miss my Paris apartment at all."

Place des Vosges, where Shubel had his pied-à-terre, "couldn't be a more different neighborhood than South of Market." But it is here he found a loft of nearly identical proportions and proceeded to create his own paradisiacal corner of France, with help from many of the pieces imported directly from his former apartment. Measuring 1,200 square feet, the two-story space was a great big "brown box"—bittersweet chocolate from floor to ceiling with turquoise accents—"definitely not my colors," he says, wincing. Nearly brand new, it required nothing prior to decorating except gallons and gallons of white paint to bring forward the furnishings' nuances and help create his ethereal, airy home. He splashed it everywhere, stopping only at the oak planks beneath his feet—he was ready to paint them too, when at the last moment he realized a white floor would require constant care to maintain a fresh appearance.

"I gravitate toward silhouettes," says Shubel, and this penchant is evident in the foyer. Matisse-inspired upholstery, overlapping cowhide rugs—a favorite floor covering because "they don't make you feel like you're getting into or out of a different space"—and the charcoal painting by Amy Sollins above the desk are cases in point. Far from being a snob when it comes to defining his vision, Shubel will use any material that suits his purpose, regardless of its worth. He found awning-striped cotton online for eight dollars per yard, in one instance, promptly using it to upholster an eighteenth-century Swedish daybed. The 17-foot-high living room/workspace, brilliant with sunlight reflected by the wall of antique mirrors, contains an equally interesting compilation of furnishings. The sofa acted as his bed in Paris; and the resin side table found its way next to it because of its hoofed legs—animal touches are another of the designer's predilections. The real scene-stealer, however, is the goddess Juno who presides over the far end of the room. Fashioned of plaster, she is a rarity; "I've never seen another," he says, "and plan to hold onto her forever."

Behind her is the terrace; its hedge mimics those in the Palace of Versailles gardens, but is plastic, with a few real plants mingled among the leaves. The charade usually fools people, at least from a distance. Lighthearted as well as all business, Shubel transformed the "box-within-a-box" bathroom into a trompe l'oeil circus tent with painted stripes. A world apart in design from the rest of his home, it is useful for more than its primary purpose. He hides a washer, dryer, and office paraphernalia behind its curtain, maximizing the utility of the space. Perhaps even more important, he says, eyes twinkling, "Clients walk out smiling."

French in another life or not—he jokes it could be possible—Shubel ends the day in his bedroom *à la français*, going so far as to hang the paintings along the bottom of the wall so he can see them from bed.

"It's like Marie Antoinette in a T-shirt . . . the past recreated for today."

There was so much wrong about the cottage when I bought it," remembers Shubel, "it really frightened people." He's six-foot-two and the ceilings hover at seven-and-a-half feet; the very uneven floors needed to be leveled; heating and plumbing systems required updating; and the bathrooms were falling apart. But he saw its charm, seals could be heard barking at the shore and foghorns bellowed at night. No doubt in his mind, this was it.

The designer, who didn't want color at home after thinking about it all week long, lightened the interior by painting the original tongue-in-groove redwood paneling a pure white. "But it was too bright," says Shubel. Unable to live with it for a minute, he returned to the store for an ivory shade, using it and the striped floor treatment to unify the living and dining areas. He finds black and white comfortable to live with, but the right balance is mandatory, he cautions—too much black can give a room a cold, harsh feel while the correct amount will provide a warm, inviting one. He also judged that a great deal of black could inflict a citified air, and he was adamant about retaining the house's fundamental seafaring character. The last important factor was practicality: papillons Coco and Lulu accompany Shubel wherever he goes so easy care was essential.

The interior décor is all about imbuing fine antiques with a relaxed attitude, which Shubel accomplishes with everyday ticking and sailcloth upholstery, and surprises like the numbers he stenciled on the Louis XVI chairs—guests are asked to seat themselves by picking their favorite. The sort of cook who reads five recipes for a dish and then concocts his own version, preparing meals for friends is one of his greatest delights, and fun to do here in his high-performance kitchen.

Shubel uses enough nautical touches to remind visitors of their whereabouts, although some, like the first floor's grommeted, denim window shades, are subtle. His playful way of combining pieces from a variety of sources, however, is often the first thing visitors notice. A Roman urn leads the way to the stairs, its handrail made of sailing rope. The wide-striped, black-and-white fabric covering some pillows and capping a bedroom stool were made from priests' robes bought at an old French church's "closing the doors" sale. He stacks a mound of reading material on a naïve, leather fisherman's chair encompassed by serious pieces dating from the 1800s. Whimsical elegance is Shubel's signature, and even in this most unexpected setting, he succeeds in creating a space with a complete confidence of style that is decidedly French.

MICHAEL BERMAN

LOS ANGELES, CALIFORNIA & PALM SPRINGS, CALIFORNIA

From the midcentury houses he shares with life partner Lee Weinstein it's easy to see that Michael Berman loves the 1960s. Sitting high in the Hollywood Hills, their primary residence is "a luxurious place to crash" after long days on the job during the week. It epitomizes serenity, although Berman is constantly moving things around. Similarly furnished, but different in mood due to its breezy, uninterrupted floor plan, their Palm Springs home is designed for lazy days with friends and reading by the pool.

"There's a feeling of formality here, but it's also cozy."

Get right over here, Lee, I found us a house," Michael Berman recalls saying to his partner. Driving around Los Feliz, his favorite neighborhood and one that rarely has anything on the market, he spied a "For Sale" sign. The house was everything he wanted: a two-bedroom, horseshoe-shaped ranch situated on a corner lot with views of the ocean, Griffith Observatory, and downtown Los Angeles. As luck would have it—or perhaps fate—and unbeknownst to him at the time, it dated from 1964, his favorite year for its furniture, music, and cars.

"Lightly lived in" by one couple for forty years, the residence was in a marvelous time warp: nearly everything mint, down to the wall-mounted, rotary phone in the breakfast room. "It was as though it had been preserved for us," says Berman. Sharing this thought with the owner and promising he would not gut it, he and Lee Weinstein were soon signing on the dotted line. Berman's intent was not to erect a monument to the 1960s, but to enhance the house's architectural integrity and make the most of its location. The first step was to prepare a blank canvas with soft ecru walls. A "clean" background, he says, makes it possible to combine several styles as he did here—including 1960s and 1970s American and 1970s

Italian—and allows them to have a dialogue with each other. Avoiding clutter, he adds, helps to create the visual continuum from object to object and room to room needed for a relaxed atmosphere.

Old-time Hollywood chic shows up in funky patterns and elliptical shapes, and especially in Berman's use of light-reflecting materials. First in his design book is vinyl. And he uses it extensively, even to upholster his bed's headboard. He creates more gleam, softly, with the 1970s polished-aluminum light fixture and patent-leather-and-lacquer chairs in the breakfast room and Monteverdi Young trapezoidal table in the living room. Tying the look together is the flooring, much of it silver travertine tiles. Of course, there is also some out-and-out razzle-dazzle: the glamorous master bath, suggestive of those in Doris Day and Rock Hudson movies, is lit with chandeliers that once glittered in Zsa Zsa Gabor's home.

"Houses should mirror their residents," Berman says, "and this one does—neat, straightforward, comfortable. Plus it's in a convenient location." Relax? There's the pool. Theater? Hollywood Boulevard is fifteen minutes away. A run with Fritz the basenji? Griffith Park is around the bend.

"The minute the San Jacinto Mountains come into view,
my blood pressure drops and a sense of calm descends."

Look for the *Wizard of Oz* emerald-green door," says Berman, his standard directions. This time a broker friend saw the house first, and made a mental note that it was quintessentially Berman: a mid-century ranch built in 1964, with the type of circular drive he coveted. The very next day the owner happened to call, inquiring if he knew of anyone that might be interested. "This is an architectural gem," says Berman of his home, "inspired by the 'glass box' styling of the 1960s Case Study houses."

The biggest deterrent to readying it was the weather: 118-degree desert temperatures meant truncated work days, but over a three-month period, everything came together. Most essential was unifying the entire living area into one free-flowing space by replacing the hodgepodge of floor coverings with poured terrazzo. Small windows morphed into great expanses of glass and everything, including the exterior, received coats of creamy white paint. Berman turned to the "martini era" for inspiration—that of Frank Sinatra and the Rat Pack—beginning on the terrace side of the room. Somewhat like a 1960s conversation pit, it holds an inviting curve of modern furniture: a boomerang-shaped sectional, a 1970s Milo Baughman chaise longue tucked near the fireplace, and a pair of Warren Platner chairs from 1966 that still wear their original green, worsted wool—possibly the only seating in the house on which damp bathing suits are taboo.

"Treasure hunting is my weekend exercise," Berman jokes. And he takes chances with anything he's drawn to: humble, pricey, serious, or wacky. The black-and-white painting in the living room is a good example. It was yellow from cigarette smoke when he saw it at a sale, but he thought with a little cleaning it would complement his other, colorful art. So he bought it. A few hours scrubbing the canvas with a toothbrush proved his hunch correct, and up it went. He couldn't walk away from the fiberglass horse heads either. He turned these movie props into a Hollywood Regency–style table, perfect for serving hors d'oeuvres.

Leading the way to the master bedroom—where Robin Mitchell's pastel provides a dash of color, and occasional tables that belonged to Ginger Rogers add a soupçon of glamour—Berman pauses at the iron, circa 1870 Anglo-Indian raj table. "It's lucky because of the upturned elephant trunks," he explains, smiling knowingly. It stood solo for a long time when, seemingly out of nowhere, the delicate "stiletto-style" corner chairs came to Berman's attention, allowing the group to be positioned for an evening tête-à-tête. Fate again?

Whether it's toasting s'mores around a bonfire in the hills, barbecuing for friends, or getting back to nature in the spiritual tranquility of the desert, Berman says, "This is the perfect place to chill."

MOLLY LUETKEMEYER

LOS ANGELES, CALIFORNIA & MONTECITO, CALIFORNIA

Bold colors and dramatic graphics caught Molly Luetkemeyer's eye early on. By age seven she was already voicing her opinions on her mother's decorating style. Today, people take her ideas more seriously. Luetkemeyer lives in a 1950s house perched in the hills north of Los Angeles that dances with Mediterranean colors, and brings to mind an island vacation. On the weekends she takes refuge in a serene little cabin in the Montecito woods whose decorative scheme was inspired by the pastels she admired when she visited Jaipur, the Pink City of India.

"It's a movable feast. I like changing things around to see how the sun affects them."

Don't even think about Laurel Canyon—it's not right at all," Luetkemeyer remembers telling the broker. But, she says, "Luckily, he ignored me. I fell in love with the house the moment I walked up to it." Apologizing for the cliché, she describes the site as "magical," with its flowering crape myrtle, hummingbirds flitting by, and pair of resident owls. The 1,500-square-foot deck that essentially doubles the living space and projects over the hill like a ship's prow was the final enticing detail that convinced her to buy the house. She immediately envisioned what needed to be done to the interior: reorient the bedroom and adjoining bath for more natural light, spruce up the kitchen, and lay wood flooring. These relatively easy fixes allowed her to move in quickly.

A floor-to-ceiling mural inspired by Henri Rousseau's jungle paintings is the focal point of an entry sequence that stretches the length of the house. Bold strokes continue in the living room, which exemplifies her technique of blending circles and squares, solids and patterns. Round leather Moroccan poufs—footrests for adults and unending sources of amusement for visiting nieces and nephews—inject an exotic note. The Art Deco shapes of the vanilla corduroy-covered chairs add a curve to the room's many squared-off elements, and begin its theme of black-and-white against bright tropical colors that continues with the 1930s alabaster lamps and rug.

Large gatherings on the deck are Luetkemeyer's favorite summertime entertainment, but come winter, smaller indoor dinner parties retain a festive, warm-weather aura under the dining room's striped ceiling inspired by Italian beach cabanas. Friends can linger on Hans Wegner's 1949 wishbone chairs, which surround an oval ebonized dining table and rest on top of a zebra rug whose stripes echo the strong graphic pattern above. The kitchen resembles a ship's galley—everything is flush, down to the drawer pulls. "The last thing you want in a small space," she cautions, "is to be jabbed unexpectedly." The floating cabinet that allows her colorful collection of glassware to be on permanent display and ocean-colored tile that changes with the light complete the feel.

Fascinated by the interplay of its bold colors, she upholstered her bedroom walls in an exuberant flower pattern. "Why not?" Luetkemeyer asks. "I find it soothing and didn't have to talk someone else into agreeing with me about the choice." Neutrals are used to temper the vibrant walls—beginning with the luxuriously supple ivory cowhide rugs on the floor. Subtle metallic vinyl wraps the headboard, an inexpensive option that reflects light and reads like leather. "I'd love to be an artist in my next incarnation," she muses. For now she's a collector, buying what she likes as she sees it, unconcerned about where it might go. As with a Maria von Köhler resin-and-wax bull's head, her approach can produce surprising results. Remembering this particular composite's humidity-resistant properties, she hung the sculpture unexpectedly in the bathroom.

"I think about working here, but I never do; it's too peaceful."

Luetkemeyer's cornflower blue cabin seems like an unlikely choice for a recording studio, but this is precisely what its previous owner, Kenny Loggins, used it for. "I believe a lot of creative energy is still here—one of the things I find special about it," says the designer. She knew an overhaul would be necessary to make the A-frame structure livable; it possessed a few too many electrical outlets and partitioning glass doors—carryovers from music production—for starters. She also knew she could carve its 1,000 square feet into a home perfect for one, creating a living room, bedroom, small kitchen, and bath. The shower, however, can be found out back, hidden by a discreet bamboo hedge.

Planned for barefoot informality, Luetkemeyer's cabin brings to mind the rhythmic patterns and soft colors of India within a context of timber and stone. The pairing sounds improbable, but succeeds thanks to her many artistic touches. In homage to Indian design's capacity to embrace both local and European styles and patterns, she selected a combination of furnishings based on a variety of elements—old-fashioned curves and streamlined contemporary shapes, origin, and overall appearance. The living room exhibits this happy mix in its juxtaposition of traditional, like the sofa with its Victorian tendencies, and modern, like the mirrored side tables and midcentury Italian chairs. And while the gold-leafed lamps hail from Summerland—a nearby town famous for surfing as well as antique shops—and the hassock is Moroccan, they exhibit the same spirit as the textiles from the subcontinent. At the other end of the room is a daybed Luetkemeyer commissioned, painted a pink often seen in Kashmiri shawls. Lit from above by a cut-brass lantern from Udaipur, it is a favorite spot for reading and napping. It can also be pressed into service for overnight guests.

Her own bedroom brings nature inside with peeled wood timbers rubbed with paint that draw the eye to the small clerestory window, a half wall of freeform stones as a rustic interpretation of wainscoting, and wood-plank floor. "Lying in bed under the skylight, able to see the stars and hear the birds, is the most wonderful way to end the day," she says. "I'll be here until I outgrow it... whenever that might be."

BARCLAY BUTERA

NEWPORT BEACH, CALIFORNIA & PARK CITY, UTAH

He might look like a surfer, but Barclay Butera's focus is on fabrics and furniture, rather than the Wedge, and it's the refined elegance and classical tailoring of 1940s couture that inspire him. Butera, whose second passion is real estate, downsized from five houses—one of which was Frank Sinatra's Palm Springs home—to the two he loves most. His primary residence in Newport Beach is country club classic, with gleaming mahogany and patterns galore. Six hundred miles away in Park City, Utah, Butera lets his inner cowboy out, roping in a Western motif with art and antiques.

"I've learned to slow down here and appreciate what I have."

Southern California has been Butera's base for much of his life, so this 1950s ranch house in Newport Beach appealed to him for a number of reasons: "It's on a huge double lot, rare in these parts," he explains, "and only three miles from the office. My design team is like family. We work together *and* play together. This is an easy drive for everyone to make for dinner and a soak in the jacuzzi."

With entertaining in mind, Butera decided on an open plan for the 2,700-square-foot space. He began by ripping out the bathrooms, reconfiguring beams and ceilings, and installing new cabinetry. Only then did he turn to the décor, immersing the house in an ocean of blues and whites. "It reminds me of the seaside," he says, finding it "comforting to know it's so close by." But this is no typical beach cottage— although there are seashells depicted in numerous antique nature prints on the walls, unusual coral specimens topping books on many tables, and a giant clam shell used as a planter in one of the guest bedrooms. The two-tone color scheme is repeated in each room of the house, but Butera varies the mood by introducing a range of furnishings, textures, and patterns. The dining area borders on formal, its audacious mix of toile de Jouy, stripes, and Chinese porcelains set off

smartly by the ebony-stained floor and mahogany chairs of his design. The living room is relaxed with a sofa from his eponymous retail collection, a bamboo fire screen scooped up at a flea market, and leopard-print carpeting. And the family room that opens onto the garden feels easy as a picnic with lots of sea grass, rattan, and the nearly ceiling-high, batten board wainscoting. Butera's office evokes a different atmosphere still: all-business in sedate stripes and Scottish plaid. The designer's vision of carefree glamour embraces every room.

Butera collects such vintage silver pieces as clocks, flasks, and ashtrays, tucking them among favorite books on the shelves in his office, and displaying them elsewhere in the house. He also went wild with wallpaper, one of his favorite decorative tools, hanging fourteen different types throughout, including one made of raffia on the family room ceiling. The last step of the renovation was landscaping. "I live in the garden," he says, "and love to entertain on the terrace." His favorite type of get-together? Potluck-style dinners, especially when everyone brings a homemade specialty. "That way we can all have fun, and no one is stuck with clean-up— especially me!" he jokes.

"The smell of the pines, crackling fireplace, friends

and family to share it with . . . what's not to love?"

I've admired Park City since I skied here as a kid," says Butera. "It's changed greatly since then, but it's still a far cry from Newport Beach." A quick drive to the airline hub of Salt Lake City, which makes flying to either coast for client meetings a snap, it offers many of the activities he enjoys year-round, from mountain biking in the summer to the Sundance Film Festival in the winter. Butera bought the loft for its notable location at the edge of a creek, surrounded by Aspen trees, yet only 50 feet from Main Street, bustling with restaurants and boutiques. Under the pitched ceiling that soars to 18 feet at its apex, the two bedrooms, vast great room, and open kitchen reveal his design concept: an inviting interior that reflects the singular colors of the mountains and sky, sunrise and sunset. Multiple patterns, including seemingly discordant paisleys, stripes, Jacobean prints, and American Indian blanket motifs combine with fabrics and rugs in a slew of textures.

As befits an ideal mountain retreat, the rooms display lots of buttery-soft leather, old-timey trunks and horns—big, curvy examples from a Texas long-horn shape a hide-covered chair in his bedroom; sun-bleached deer antlers are placed like sculpture on armoires; and those of an elk twist and turn into a lamp near the fireplace. But Butera being Butera, he enhances the cowpoke aesthetic with glimpses of his cattle baron side. "Just because you wear jeans and cowboy boots," he insists, "doesn't mean you have to forgo elegance." His touch of chic is quiet: Some of the trunks are vintage Louis Vuitton, Chinese porcelains add grace to the rustic surroundings, and a number of the antique pocket watches he collects are on display. With a few paintings, the house is complete. "Look at this one," he says, indicating William "Royden" Card's *Guardian at Katherine* hanging in the red master bedroom. "It's like Utah itself. It brings you back to reality, if even for a short period of time."

PAM DUNCAN

SANTA FE, NEW MEXICO & TRES LAGUNAS, NEW MEXICO

"Santa Feans are collectors," says Pam Duncan, and her many displays of unique, handcrafted objects make it clear that she is one of the most astute among them. Contemporary art glass, Hispanic folk art, textiles, and early Americana are her passion, and she integrates them all into the homes she shares with husband Donn Duncan. During the week, it's a Pueblo Revival house nestled in the foothills of the Jemez Mountains. Formal yet lighthearted, it hums with color, much of it from artwork. When the snow melts, the couple heads to a log cabin in the tiny community of Tres Lagunas for long weekends. Here, antique sporting equipment, prints, and artifacts from different periods and origins add to the cabin's inherent charm.

"We hear birds singing, coyotes howling, nature's close by. It's low-key and easy to live in."

Duncan is brave. She not only weaves together an international mix of furnishings, accessories, and fabrics into her personalized Santa Fe style, she stayed put during the two-and-a-half-year renovation of her home. That turned out to be the easy part. It was the living room décor that proved troublesome. "The sun is so intense here," she explains, "it's not only uncomfortable on the eyes, it drains color of its vitality. And I certainly don't like keeping the draperies pulled tight."

With her artistic sensibility, she solved both problems by turning to a natural linen color palette that tempers the glare. It also has the effect of directing attention to densely saturated splashes of accent color, such as an early-twentieth-century Margaret Bruton painting near the window, the silk-covered, late-nineteenth-century chairs and, most notably, her art glass collection. Displayed in a 12-foot-long glass vitrine, the vivid works of Dale Chihuly, William Morris, Ginny Ruffner, and Preston Singletary catch the sun's glinting rays and are transformed into a functional element of the décor. The case also serves as a spectacular wall for the corridor that leads to the dining room.

Old World touches—a French Régence mirror and Spanish fireplace chair that still wears its original velvet-and-leather upholstery—add romance. Duncan brings it down to earth with finds like the English wheelwright's table, and references the house's location by incorporating such elements as the Afghan and Oushak rugs intimating the muted shades of New Mexico's wintertime landscape.

The joy she derives from using her abilities to create harmonic rhythms of even the most diverse elements is seen in the guest bedrooms. Classic toile and Persian-style paisleys join the carved and painted Latin furniture for spare elegance in the first. It's French provincial quilts and brass bed frames painted blue and Guatemalan stripes brightened by *mola* appliqué in the second. "Call it kitschy," Duncan laughs, "it's where all out-of-towners, even my kids and grandkids, want to stay." Some of the work here, like the tin-framed prints by leading *santero* Charlie Carillo are serious pieces. Others—there are Mexican redware roosters and clay pigs—are simply great fun. "Whether they have monetary value, aesthetic merit or both," Duncan explains, "I find them amazing examples of the art around us."

"I catch the lazy fish… those that don't get up 'til nine in the morning."

Twelve miles as the crow flies" is the distance between Duncan's front door in Santa Fe and her log cabin near the banks of the Pecos River, where elk and bears amble down for a drink at dusk. The idea of owning a vacation home had long been percolating in her mind, as well as her husband's, an avid fly fisherman, and finally became a reality after visiting a client in this area about which she knew very little. "It was simply enchanting," she reminisces. On the grounds of a circa 1910 ranch, the 1,600-square-foot cabin is the perfect display environment for many of her favorite collectibles, which had been previously stored away.

Before starting in on the design, Duncan built a second-floor porch for viewing the mountains, finished the upstairs ceilings with narrow *latilla* logs, and brightened the kitchen with new cabinet and counter finishes. In keeping with the woodsy setting and to ensure visits from friends and family are free from worry about damaging valuable pieces or delicate materials, she devised an unpretentious look her husband calls "Aunt Hattie style." The comfortable patina she developed begins with the textiles—washable Stewart plaid upholstery that complements the stone fireplace and "grays down" the yellow undertone of the fir *viga* logs, and Tibetan rugs that provide contrasting pattern.

"I don't set out to buy off-beat things," Duncan says, "but when something like the aluminum fishing creel from World War II comes to my attention, I pounce." Relics from the 1880s through the 1940s and furniture made of hickory saplings give every room an old-fashioned feel. A 1920s gun rack in the dining room embellished with a fishing net and antique rifle continues the motif, and unusual rustic lamps, including a standing version made of a fist-thick grapevine in the living room and table lamps fashioned from French and Mexican candlesticks in the bedrooms, come as pleasant surprises. Filling in the space beneath the split-log staircase is an Italian chest she had painted with a traditional, Guatemalan squiggly-comb pattern. The loft, which visiting children draw straws to win the privilege of sleeping in, also gets a Central American touch with carved wood dance masks above the closet.

Duncan's life on the river differs from the one she leads in Santa Fe as much as the two homes differ from each other. "It's fun to cook here," she says, allowing her to forget work. She reads under the shade of the giant cottonwood trees surrounding the house, falls asleep to the pitter-patter of evening rain and never, ever gets up at dawn—no matter how good the fishing.

HANDTIED FLIES AND LURES

JOHN PHIFER MARRS

DALLAS, TEXAS & EUREKA SPRINGS, ARKANSAS

"Eureka Springs, Arkansas is not exactly a hot spot for designers," jokes John Phifer Marrs, referring to the small town close to where he grew up. "To be in this field you have to move to the big city." So he did, landing in Dallas. His house there offers simple elegance within an environment of fine art and antiques, inherited pieces and numerous collections. But every six weeks or so, he returns to his roots for a 360-degree change of pace. Hanging off the side of a hilly peninsula, his cottage is strewn with a jumble of florals and comfortable furnishings that invite nothing more strenuous than reading a good book.

"I love my work, but there is much more to life than that."

wanted some land," says Marrs, who had been living in downtown Dallas. And he found it, ten miles from the city's center. Situated on half an acre in a 1950s-era neighborhood, the 2,700-square-foot ranch house is shaded by enormous old oaks. The house had not been significantly updated since 1956, which meant some changes were in order. Some were fast and relatively uncomplicated—the hardwood floors, which had been carpeted for all those years, simply required refinishing. Others were slow and more involved—the kitchen, dusty rose in color from vinyl floor to Formica countertops, demanded a complete redo.

Once Marrs assigned each room a function— the room receiving floods of morning light lending itself to the idea of coffee and newspapers, for example, became the study—and had the main color scheme decided, it was on to composition. "I move things around until they look right and there's something lovely to see from every angle," he explains. Comfort is also crucial and he adds it with panache, placing a sinuous 1880s wicker chaise in the family room, and raising the dining table on casters to give tall guests extra legroom. A rarely mentioned asset among interior designers is patience, and Marrs has plenty. "Better to wait than get it wrong," he believes, relaying how it took ten years and the

perusal of hundreds of swatches to find the harlequin fabric that now covers the nineteenth-century chairs in the study. "It was absolutely worth the wait," he says. "It strikes just the right chord: unpretentious with a dollop of humor."

Southern to the core, the designer appreciates many of his furnishings as much for their sentimental as artistic or monetary merit. The French balloon prints, displayed on either side of the breakfront that shows off his Parian and transferware were a housewarming gift. One of his first important purchases, the 1860s marquetry chest in the living room, anchors two Joan Mirós and a Henri de Toulouse-Lautrec engraving. And the 1930s secretary—a reproduction gaming chair angled in front—was inherited from his grandmother. Another lesson in patience, it took a year to restore. But the handpainted, bird's-eye-maple-and-ebony design turned the "plain cousin" into a "raving beauty."

Marrs loves giving parties. "I'm not the greatest cook," he says, "but I know how to make a good presentation." He starts guests off in the piano room, serving hors d'oeuvres and drinks on the marble-topped Charles X table. Then, at the appointed hour, he throws open the doors to the dining room and its exquisitely set table—pure drama! "Like dinner parties from my childhood," he says, "no one ever wants to leave."

"The house's peninsula site makes it feel like a ship in the middle of the ocean."

By the time Marrs arrives at "Camp Laughing Bear," he's relaxed, with his sole concern any progress that might have been made by the local population of red-headed woodpeckers that sometimes mistake his house for a delicious snack. Their signature hammer marks and the need for a new roof were the only imperfections he found when he came upon it several years ago. He was more than ready to overlook these for its two guest bedrooms and the location—an easy ten-minute trip from the town's grocery stores, art galleries, and restaurants.

His plan was to play up the contrast between this house and his Dallas home, or as he jokes, "create a cozy cottage with a place to nap in every room." A finely tuned composition of multiple furniture styles tied together with reds, greens, and florals makes the space feel as if it has been there for generations. And nearly everything has a story: Marrs's mother repainted the living room's catalog-issue lamps because the colors were slightly off; the eyes of the woman in the nineteenth-century portrait above the sofa seem to follow guests' every move, something the designer finds amusing; and the side tables in his red bedroom are actually the rounded ends of an antique dining table.

Coming in from the dining room where he serves meals on fine bone china paired with inexpensive straw placemats, Marrs says that decorating his first vacation home made him appreciate the importance of using only furnishings and materials that are washable or dustable. To that end the slipcovers are sturdy polished cotton, the window shades are bamboo, and the porch's industrial carpet can be hosed down. But that doesn't preclude luxurious items. Luckily, as the only member of the family interested in antiques, he inherited many pieces—grandmother's 1880 china cupboard and Victoriana—that pair well with his own finds, even the Napoleon III–style chair and carved Bavarian benches.

While he decorates instinctively, reasoning bolsters every decision. Why is the painting to the left of the bookcase unframed? He likes its "primitive elegance," and it keeps the house from looking "too designed." The painted screen that is reminiscent of a gypsy wagon? It gives dimension to the room. So much packed into his bedroom? Large items like king-size beds need ballast. Logic is an essential tool in decorating . . . whether to please the eye or make living more comfortable.

"Every house should be full of things that make you smile," concludes Marrs. This house clearly is.

RENEA ABBOTT

HOUSTON, TEXAS & AUSTIN, TEXAS

Contrast defines Renea Abbott's design style: pattern on solid, shine against matte, antique with contemporary. It also characterizes her life: a nonstop whirl of work, fun, casual dinners, and gala fund-raisers. She lives with her husband Greg Manteris in a new townhouse in an old Houston neighborhood. Predominantly black and white, accented with silver and gold, it's 1930s glamour gone modern. Come Thursday afternoon, Lake Austin calls. Their second home is elegantly informal, sporting horn furniture and rare sightings of "leopard." Indoors, outdoors. Stilettos or sneakers. Both are polished to perfection.

"I like seeing my guests' reaction the first time they walk into the black living room!"

We snuck through the gates of the construction site and raced through the house," remembers Abbott. "Then we called the realtor for the price." Located in the city's leafy Museum District, the Mediterranean-style residence is minutes to her shop and the Rice University track. "That sealed the deal for Greg," says Abbott. Once the couple's offer was accepted, they asked the builder to stop work. The house was nearly three-quarters finished: too late to avoid numerous built-ins and bathrooms not to their taste, which they later redid, but in time to avoid the contractor's choice of flooring and paint.

Strolling past the stairway lined with Helmut Newton photographs and into the living room, Abbott plunks down on a love seat, citing the Black Bar at Hôtel Costes in Paris—another place she snuck into, undeterred by its closed status on the day of her visit—as its inspiration. Black was new to her, but she forged ahead knowing the sun pouring in through the windows would highlight the wallpaper's geometric pattern; and the mirrors would reflect the candles and lamplight in the evening. Plus, white and cream abound—the muslin upholstery, Reuben Nakian painting, bleached oak floors—as do the twinkles from a crystal chandelier and metal accent pieces. Explaining her theory about glamorous environments, Abbott points to the pair of antique French mirrors: "Sometimes too much is just enough. These work because they *are* so dramatic; anything simpler wouldn't stand up to the wallpaper."

While saving serious cooking for weekends at the lake, Abbott does have a great little dining nook in the kitchen here. It's glamorous, too: silk-velvet, zebra-print cushions on curvy chairs found at a French flea market and Calcutta gold, marble-faced walls. The upstairs presents quite a different appearance, reflecting the monochromatic glamour of early movies. An enormous Russian Empire chandelier measuring 54 inches in height is the most eye-catching accessory in an otherwise subtly decorated master bedroom and sitting room suite—crystal lamps, simple but powerful artwork, and the abundant use of pearl-hued silk and mohair add elegance.

"Every room needs some drama. It makes it more fun."

Decidedly outdoorsy, Abbott was boating with friends on Lake Austin when she noticed a new house rising in the distance. "The next thing you know," she relates, "we're in the car going for a closer look." The setting reminded her of Portofino, Italy, built as it is into a hill with steps leading 20 feet down to the crystal-clear water. Ten spacious rooms, a view preserved for many years to come thanks to building restrictions, an outdoor dining room with a fireplace for grilling, and a pool made it obvious: the perfect vacation home. Within weeks she and Manteris were driving a 26-foot-long moving van to Austin.

"This is my first attempt at using soft, pretty colors for myself," she says. "I thought it would be calming and a good foil for the little twist of Hollywood I always put in." Guests receive a peek at her style before they even enter the house—an Art Deco, leopard-spotted chair and 1830s, four-paned German mirror are visible through a front window. Bathed in sunlight, the living room seating is simply upholstered in humble muslin, "furniture's undergarment," as Abbott calls it. The accoutrements add the grandeur.

Overtly, of course, there are the animal prints, fox throw, and a zebra-seated chair formed entirely of elk horns. There are also more refined flourishes, such as the sparkling convex mirrors that bring attention to two panels of Ford Beckman's squares-on-squares triptych, and gold frames bordering Reuben Nakian's work above the fireplace. One of the frames is made in a broken-mitered format—expensive looking, but actually not, because gilded frames are sold by the foot. Abbott plays it both ways in the heavily-trafficked family room between kitchen and dining terrace. The patterns and flashy, goat-skin-covered stools may seem exotic touches for such a functional space, but everything was selected for a reason: the two-toned rug takes wear well, and the stools are handy "pull-ups" for extra seating. In comparison, the upstairs sitting room is almost monastic, Texas-style. The little horn lamp is a favorite for its unusual crinoline-like shade; so is her husband's coffee table, one of the pieces he brought to the marriage.

"The guest room is always full, we water ski and wakeboard, and on Saturday nights we have family-style feasts! I couldn't ask for more," smiles Abbott.

BEVERLY JACOMINI

HOUSTON, TEXAS & ROUND TOP, TEXAS

Beverly Jacomini is a true Texan, appreciative of both past and present. Her gracious Georgian-style home in Houston glides effortlessly from today to yesterday and back again, warm and inviting, casually elegant. At her 1857 farmhouse in Round Top, the heart of bluebonnet country, intricate floral stenciling and furniture crafted by early settlers star. Seamlessly blending old with new, it is in her view the most comfortable place in the world, where she and husband Tommy Jacomini put aside the frenzied pace of work to enjoy family and friends, gardening, and swimming in the pool.

"The minute I walk in and close the door behind me, I'm in a different world."

Walking up to Jacomini's 1930s house in Houston's River Oaks neighborhood, with its sparkling white columns, two-story shuttered windows, and exquisitely landscaped grounds creates an expectation for similar grandeur inside. All it takes is entering through the front door to find it, Jacomini-fashion.

Inside, a 40-foot-long checkered entrance hall of oak planks painted to resemble marble and decorated with a pair of iron lemon trees—antiques from turn-of-the-century France—leads to a living room with walls splashed in a surprising glossy tomato red.

"Tommy thought I was bonkers," Jacomini remembers when she told her husband the plan. "But he decided that he loved it even before the paint dried." A few years later, when the couple annexed the adjacent utility room to accommodate their growing family, they realized that views from two of the room's windows would be blocked. Her clever solution? Build bookshelves over them, and keep the shutters on the interior, but paint them white to match the rest of the room's trim. In addition to the white trim, which prevents the abundance of red from becoming overwhelming, accent patterns on the carpet and elsewhere serve as a visual divider between walls and seating. The installation of a gracefully arched, glass-paned door between the living room and entry hall, and an extra large pass-through—designed with shutters so it can be closed off when the kitchen becomes too noisy—between it and the family room, also helped to partition the 4,500-square-foot house into segments that can promote togetherness and provide an elegant ambience for entertaining.

As can be seen at every turn, Jacomini believes in mixing styles for both appearance and function. In the dining room, for example, she combined plain Mexican and decorated Italian chairs around a Regency table. In the kitchen, an 1850s wine-tasting table that is the perfect size for family meals conveniently folds flat when space is needed; steel hooks from a 1920s mail train are repurposed to support her collection of copper pots and pans; and the professional range melds into the background surrounded by pine-stained cypress cabinets and a maple counter personalized with small artworks by midcentury great William Hoey, Caroline Graham, and herself.

"Living in the house such a long time," she says, "I have so many fond memories. They'll always be with me."

"This is not country with a K."

We'll take it, but we don't need the land," the Jacominis told the broker after touring this farmhouse built in 1857 in the village of Industry, an hour or so from Houston. They had it cut in half and driven on flat-bed trucks to their eighty acres in Round Top, which also happens to be the home of one of the country's most famous antiques fairs, and where the designer often scouts for clients. Upon arrival, they found the house in good shape; the wide-plank, pine walls and ceiling paint were barely marred. Even more astonishing were the well-preserved rows upon rows of decorative floral stenciling in the living and dining rooms. A ravaged roof had allowed mud to penetrate the interiors, which had to be hosed out, and bathrooms needed to be built, but once those items were struck from the agenda, Jacomini began bringing it back to life, starting with a minutely detailed floor plan. "Always important," she counsels, "but especially with old structures like this where the walls are crooked, nothing lines up, and everything is a little off."

Cooking in the country is one of the designer's greatest pleasures, using herbs and vegetables from her garden—if she can get to them faster than the hungry armadillos, that is—so her first task was to double the size of the kitchen. While in concert with the era of the house, it incorporates all the modern conveniences, including an electrified, circa-1800s wood-burning stove. In addition, since "people today are taller than the pioneers," she elevated the stove and pie safe on a platform. Jacomini applied the standards of comfort to the furniture as well. Her six-foot-tall husband tested everything before purchases were made, from their red sleigh bed to the dining chairs. "The big wooden ones might have been at Texas A&M when it opened in 1876," she says. In Jacomini's book, authenticity is important, but personal style and the aforementioned comfort are too, so if a contemporary item looks or functions better than an older object, there's no compunction about incorporating it. Sea-grass rugs replace hooked and the classic seating downstairs aligns perfectly with the antiques. At the same time, she also decorates with antique quilts and primitive rugs in a fresh way, framing and displaying them as art throughout the home.

"The truckers who moved it here told me the house was good for nothing but firewood," recalls Jacomini, laughing. "But look at it now."

LAWRENCE BOEDER

CHICAGO, ILLINOIS & ROLLING PRAIRIE, INDIANA

If a collecting gene exists, Lawrence Boeder has it. The assemblages he's built over the past many years—and keeps embellishing—define the homes he shares with wife Mary Boeder. During the week they live in a landmark Chicago row house steps from Lake Michigan. Here, his prized American art pottery, paintings, and bronzes get top billing within a less-is-more backdrop. On the weekends they're off to their log cabin in Indiana. It's an archive of Native American artifacts, baskets, and rugs with something extra: a full-size teepee on the grounds that's perfect for parties.

"If I run out of space, I may have to get another house."

We've come full circle," says Boeder, describing how he and Mary lived two blocks away from the townhouse when they were first married. "Then we moved to the suburbs as the children came along. Once they left the nest though, we came right back." Right into the 1875 Italianate house in historic Burling Row.

The layout of the two-story, 25-foot-wide home is logical. On the first floor, the living room faces the street, the dining room is in the center, and the kitchen at the back opens onto a patio. It is this straightforward plan, along with the millwork expertly renovated by the previous tenant, that causes Boeder to say, "I feel good when I walk in. It's an easy place to live." Boeder is a classicist at heart, and designed a low-key setting using gently curved furnishings, aged rugs, and timeworn wood and marble. But he also tossed in a few unexpected details like the silver-leaf dining room ceiling and faux-leopard stools in the living room, their legs also silver-leafed, for a bit of posh. He was careful to ensure, however, that none of these would draw attention away from his collections.

He adds just enough texture to keep the eye interested—the pear-wood Biedermeier chairs carved with a seashell design and patterned Oushak carpet—yet sufficiently neutral for the artwork.

Among favorites in the living room are the antique Chinese prints between the windows, 1930s American bronzes, and a pair of 1915 Dutch clay urns on the fireplace mantle. Toward the back of the room is his "altar," as Boeder jokingly refers to it: a nineteenth-century Italian curio cabinet chock-full of so many items—pottery, porcelain figurines from the 1940s, small clocks popular in France in the 1800s, and an unbelievable array of finds representing other countries and eras—it's difficult to see a common thread among them. There is one: "Each possesses a characteristic, perhaps the shape, glaze or material, that I find beautiful and inspirational," he says. The precisely arranged green Teco pottery, and one especially rare blue piece, in the dining room receives similar attention, but in its case, he finds *every* detail wonderful. "It's nearly impossible to find Teco these days," he notes, quickly adding, "nevertheless, I keep searching."

Boeder explains that he determines his choices in a rather off-hand manner. The antique mirror was simply a "good fit" for the living room fireplace; the colors of the 1920s penny rug on the dining table add "warmth" to the room; and the Old West paintings in the den remind him of the upcoming weekend in the country. "If you like it, use it," he counsels.

"If you look and listen, a house will tell you what it needs."

I t's so beautiful here," rhapsodizes Boeder, "we come most weekends, summer, fall, winter, spring." Sited on four acres of what was once a pine tree farm—coyotes, possum, and raccoons their closest neighbors—there's "lots of nothing to do," precisely the reason the Boeders enjoy it so much.

Like a young wine, the cabin showed promise when they bought it a few years ago, but nearly every inch of it needed to be aged to create a more authentic, uncontrived appearance. The floors were stained a rich honey, birch bark was used to wrap the ceiling beams "canoe-style"—with the white surface facing in—and the banister was replaced with a custom, handcrafted stair rail, each spindle unique.

As with everything Boeder collects, perfection and value are of less importance than distinguishing traits that reveal the hand of the person who made an item, something that "makes you think about the who, why, and where of it," he says. Interested in Native American crafts since his childhood in Minnesota, he was pleased to have the opportunity to move his collection from storage and put it to use. "I loved getting it all out into the light of day," he adds. The 1920s Navajo rugs are presented as art arranged over the second-floor balcony, rather than floor coverings, because pieces of this quality are very difficult to find today; and the turkey-feather headdresses, although contemporary, were handcrafted by artisans expert in the intricacies of traditional colors and beading. He acknowledges the Persian rugs scattered about stem from a different culture, but finds a harmony in the hues and motifs of both.

The designer's passion for Native American crafts extends beyond his front door to his latest and biggest acquisition, a traditional, full-size canvas teepee. Placed a short distance from the cabin, surrounded by trees, and decorated with more ethnic rugs and blankets, it measures 21 feet high and 18 feet in diameter, holds ten people comfortably, and is an amusing venue for parties. The adventuresome say it beats a hotel for overnight stays.

ALEX JORDAN

CHICAGO, ILLINOIS & PALM DESERT, CALIFORNIA

Interiors that unite the personalities of the inhabitants with the characteristics of their homes' locations are Alex Jordan's forte, and from the residences he shares with his partner, graphic artist Michael McCarthy, it's apparent he uses his own homes to perfect his techniques. Their Chicago apartment reflects the pulse of the city, with spaces both colorful and subdued, while their southern California house echoes the palette of the nearby mountains and desert. Both teem with paintings, drawings, and sculpture—the men have been passionate collectors for more than twenty-five years—grouped in arresting ways so that each piece becomes an accessible element of the room.

"There are so many wonderful decorating styles it can sometimes be difficult to choose. This one suits our lives."

Lake Michigan's Gold Coast drew Jordan and McCarthy for a number of reasons. In addition to its proximity to friends and family, shopping and restaurants, Jordan explains, "If you're right on the lake, the view at night is a big, black void. Whereas if you're in a residential area such as ours, you see a wonderful panorama of lights."

The apartment they purchased required myriad structural changes. But the potential was obvious *and* it was irresistibly located one floor above Jordan's office. He laid out a scheme that recalls the neoclassical facade of the 1926 building, jazzed it up with streamlined, Moderne architectural details, and then got to work on the finishes and furnishings. "I like living with color and wanted to experiment," he explains. But knowing what he had in mind might be problematic for McCarthy, he took care to discuss his vision clearly with pictures and samples. This worked beautifully until the walls of the public spaces actually *became* celery, with apple green trim. "You have to repaint," McCarthy told Jordan in no uncertain terms, "beginning with the trim." Jordan refused. Within just a few days, however, Jordan says, McCarthy warmed to the unconventional approach and declared "he loved it as much as I did."

The apartment exudes urbanity with such details as an aluminum-leafed hallway, cashmere-walled sitting room—admittedly a bit extravagant—and Art Deco Savonnerie carpet in the master bedroom. But Jordan also made sure to make it convenient and comfortable for spending weekends in the kitchen, switching back and forth between "foodie" shows and experimenting with new dishes he and McCarthy can serve at their frequent dinner parties. For example, the T. H. Robsjohn-Gibbings table surrounded by chairs designed by the firm expands to seat eight, eliminating the need for a separate dining area and increasing everyday living space; the window shades rise and lower via remote control; and there is plentiful but unobtrusive lighting to quickly change a room's tone to accommodate different needs.

The flowing configuration of rooms is spaciously arranged with furnishings from the eighteenth, nineteenth, and twentieth centuries. Explaining the rationale behind their selection, he says that whether straight-edged like the French Moderne bookcase in the dining area—converted into an entertainment center—or curved like the Biedermeier chair in the living room, "they are for the most part based on neoclassical forms in keeping with the architecture." Artworks await around every turn. On view in the living room alone are such prized works as a Chryssa Varda drawing, Auguste Chabaud ink drawing and Jack Tworkov gouache on paper—even a pottery tile created by Pablo Picasso. The Thai burial vessel on top of a stone column in the sitting room, and a small-scale Alberto Giacommetti figure on a living room side table increase the gallery-as-home atmosphere, the sum total of which the couple says, reflects their personalities.

"I can't imagine a better place to escape Chicago's frigid winters."

Jordan's artistic soul comes through clearly as he describes his first glimpse of Palm Desert many years ago: "I loved the stark landscape, the quality of the air, and how the Shadow Mountains to the north turned violet as the sun went down." Soon after deciding this was a place he and Michael McCarthy could go every month or so to unwind, they began house-hunting, visiting twenty homes before deciding on this one, a flat-roofed modernist stucco in a community built in 1964. They admit most buyers would have been thrilled with the recent renovations, but not them. The pair decided significant adjustments were in order to increase the feeling of being "grounded in the desert environment" and to distill the essence of the house's era.

Naturally, the extensive transformation took longer than expected. Six months to be exact. The desert shades that initially caught Jordan's attention dominate the décor, particularly the taupe used as the background color. Accents in ivory, brick, palomino, and blue complement the spare American and Scandinavian furnishings, and the gleaming limestone flooring and gauzy draperies make it feel cool and give it a laid-back yet sophisticated vacation mood.

As in Chicago, art is everywhere. Here the works on display derive many of their colors and themes from the desert, although they vary widely in origin. An abstract, three-dimensional wood construction in a guestroom is reminiscent of Native American motifs, a Victor Skrebneski photograph in the dining area brings to mind shifting desert sand, and a hollow brick made of a terra cotta similar to that used in the region's Spanish missions, which once formed part of an ancient Chinese tomb wall, greets guests atop the entry hall table.

Jordan is pleased that in the end he took the time to get the house into the condition they really wanted. One can get "cabin fever" during Chicago's long winters, he says, and the best remedy for that is the shorts-and-sandals lifestyle the men enjoy taking advantage of here: impromptu barbecues, working on the landscaping, and floating in the pool. "I often work with my business partner Dan Smieszny on projects in the desert," he says, "but I think of them as an added bonus. Doing *anything* here is enjoyable. If everything continues to align correctly and we have our way, we'll keep both our homes forever."

SUE BURGESS

CHEVY CHASE, MARYLAND & UPPERVILLE, VIRGINIA

Hearing her parents say, "We're having a party," always made Sue Burgess happy as a child; it was her task to verify everything was just so before the guests arrived. This enduring attention to detail, eloquently expressed in the interiors she designs for others, is also apparent in the residences she shares with husband Gordon Beall. During the week they're ensconced in a brick cottage in the Washington, D.C. suburb of Chevy Chase. Spare and sophisticated, it contains glimmers of antique gilt and a variety of textures that provide drama. Their weekend "farm" echoes a similar melody, and uses the site's unique play of light and shadow as a decorative element as important as the home's graceful furnishings, creating a decidedly tranquil mood.

"It's a chain reaction, a continual evolution. I bring things in, see how they work, enjoy, revise."

One would never guess by looking at Burgess and Beall's brick house that it is twice its original size, so seamlessly does the addition blend into its 1930s frame. Burgess saw the structure's possibilities from the start; the screened-in front porch was converted into an inviting entrance and the ample property was quickly slated for an addition.

Burgess "can't operate" in clutter, but she wouldn't feel comfortable in a severely contemporary setting either. Her carefully articulated ratio of Old World glamour to twenty-first-century simplicity—and one-of-a-kind pieces like the table she made by topping a gilt-wood base with an antique mirror in the living room—defines her personal aesthetic. Refined antiques of gleaming wood and parcel gilt inhabit the understated environment. Art Deco mirrors and animal touches such as sculpted sconces, fabrics, and chair legs are classics, she says, which make them appropriate for any décor. Elsewhere, earth-toned collectibles are used for embellishment, like the eighteenth-century *tôle peinte* lavabo and zinc aloe plant on the bedroom dresser—carried home from France in a suitcase, each spiky leaf individually wrapped.

Symmetry and practicality drive Burgess's design decisions, along with the occasional indulgence. She pairs several identical items, the most prominent being the living room's Italian, gilt-wood chandeliers—purchased before she had even contemplated the overall direction for the house—and 1920s bronze window grates backed in distressed mirror that flank the fireplace. Inexpensive natural sea-grass carpeting reinforces the room's calm mood. When asked about the campaign chair and stool covered in leopard-spotted silk that cost $1,000 a yard, she counters, "But it was perfect, and I needed very little."

A hallway unexpectedly carpeted in frise linen leads to the dining room and its most prominent piece, the 1640 painting by Hendrick Cornelisz van Vliet purchased to add "depth" to the softly hued space, without adding distracting pattern. A professional cleaning revealed that what initially appeared to be a man was actually a lovely lady, bejeweled in seventeenth-century splendor, a delightful surprise. Burgess knew the seeded-glass lantern would throw a delicately suffused light over the table below, and that its bubbles would eliminate the need for frequent cleaning. "Even fine antiques can be low-maintenance and certainly used for everyday living," she says. "Then again, if something is visually pleasing, it needn't fulfill a specific function."

"Once I get here I don't want to leave, except to attend horse shows."

can count on one hand the number of weekends we've *not* been here," says Burgess. When she first came across the property, she was enchanted by the rolling hills and beautiful old barns that surrounded the house, and was undaunted by the acres of blue shag carpeting and overdone window treatments that greeted her. "We'll take the house, but not the valences," she told the real estate agent, only half-joking.

For four days the painters sprayed everything white to create a clean slate. "Making it habitable was more of a pleasure than I expected," she says. "I'd forgotten what a sense of accomplishment you can get doing things like staining floors." Plus, she adds proudly, she personally built the stone wall in back of the house. As for the eclectic mix of furnishings brought from the attic in Chevy Chase, she says, "I had fun with proportion and scale, choosing many pieces to exaggerate the dimensions of a particular space for a bit of oomph."

The dining room is illuminated by the only "precious" items in the house, her father's Russian silver candelabra, and is where the couple eats even when it is only the two of them. The oak table, chosen for the way its legs and base reflect the curves of the mohair-upholstered stools, emphasizes the length of the room and the pine doors, from a nineteenth-

century French armoire, which stop just an inch short of the 9-foot ceiling, underscore its height. Similarly, the mirror above the fireplace is of French origin. In pieces when she discovered it at Paris's Porte de Clignancourt flea market, the dealer promised he would assemble it for her, but delivered it to her hotel in the same fragmented condition. "I was on my way home," she recalls, "and wasn't about to leave it there. No worry. There are marvelous craftsmen here who handle that type of repair." Two more examples of her adept handling of proportion and scale include the master bedroom's two-paneled hanging—hand-painted on antique silk—and the four-foot-tall lamp from the 1950s, both of which highlight the room's verticality. "The trend is back to big lamps like that," she adds.

To Burgess, the "how" not the "what" creates interesting design, which oftentimes means using a piece in an unconventional way or creating a mix of high- and low-end pieces. In the living room the metal stool used as both cocktail table and extra seating was found in a popular catalog, while the parchment-covered trunk's provenance is uncertain, and the junk shop chair's linen upholstery hides its unattractive chunky legs while enhancing its overall form. "If something looks good," counsels Burgess, "it is good."

ERIC COHLER

NEW YORK, NEW YORK & CHARLESTON, SOUTH CAROLINA

Art collector, historic preservationist, palm reader. Interior designer Eric Cohler wears many hats, all at rakish angles. His company's headquarters are in New York City—which he says, "is good for work but an imposition on the soul." His haven of solitude during the week is a cleverly converted, glass-walled former office space dense with art. To relax he heads toward Charleston, South Carolina. Here, the art that enlivens the eighteenth-century house and serves as a vivid backdrop to frequent entertaining is presented as a series of careful exclamation points. Cohler's curatorial approach to interior design appears in both houses, each clearly developed for distinct lifestyles.

"It's a fortress mentality. I recharge here and get ready to do battle the next day."

Everyone called me mad for wanting this space," says Cohler, "but I bought it anyway." An extensive renovation later, and the onetime office space he had come to refer to as the "wreck with a capital W" was transformed into his refuge from the outside world. Its 1,600 square feet are spread over two floors, making it feel more like a real home than an apartment, an important feature for him. The imposing, two-story glass wall in the open living/dining area became an ideal plane for the display of art—Cohler suspends his collection in front of it on slender, industrial metal cables. A scrimlike shade filters the direct sunlight and creates privacy for cherished at-home downtime.

Cohler is his own most difficult client. "It's easier to know what's right for another person than for yourself," he contends. So he approached the duplex as though it were a design laboratory, curating his collections of art, photography, and furniture as he would a museum, planting jots of color amid neutrals. "It's all about bursts of flavors that come out when least expected," says the designer. An impressive Jacob Kainen painting creates a strong focal point in the library, for example. Noting the many patterns, especially of the furnishings downstairs and in the photos upstairs, he explains that subtle contrasts between light and dark hues make them tend to dissolve into one another, creating a visual effect similar to a solid.

Cohler's acquisitions are arranged with military precision starting at the front door with a stone sculpture by Anita Huffington. The staircase immediately to the right—with a railing wrapped in leather à la Hermès—is lined with dozens of photographs taken by such icons as Diane Arbus, Henri Cartier-Bresson, and Bert Stern. And a photograph of Mick Jagger perpetually startles guests when they enter the powder room, which is papered with very proper scenes of eighteenth-century Paris. In the living room, the assemblage dates from the circa 1750 heavily carved George II chair that sports a geometric-patterned seat to a David Salle diptych from 2003. Scattered about, as elsewhere in the duplex, are Han dynasty Chinese ceramics, 1940s tables, outsider art, and even a dining table from a chain store that was upgraded with a rich, wenge-colored stain. Despite the museum quality of so many of his possessions, Cohler believes strongly that "everything need not be precious."

"I sleep in different rooms depending upon the mood I'm in."

Through the Holland Tunnel, down the Jersey Turnpike, a sharp left, and I'm home," says Cohler. He goes to Charleston about every six weeks for grits and biscuits, golf and tennis, music, and the slower pace of life, although he says, "There's so much to do, I can't sit still."

The designer was not looking to buy when he drove to the area to visit friends in 2006. Within days, however, Cohler became enamored with the house they were renting while their own was undergoing renovation, especially its finely detailed millwork and the fact that it was in estate condition, simply musty and dusty. There was also another factor that caught his attention: a friendly ghost. "Except for rattling the windows and making my dog Sebastian whine," he recalls, "she seemed delightful."

The landmark, Federal-era Single House, as the style is called, is located in the historic Ansonborough neighborhood that edges Charleston Harbor. Its twelve rooms on five floors are reached via an original Cuban mahogany staircase and arranged less formally than his New York home. "I torqued each room until it was finely tuned, then added quirky items so it's left of center," he explains. "It's the surprises that make a place homey and personal." Why else would he juxtapose a hologram of Queen Elizabeth II and a framed square of three-dollar wrapping paper on the period fireplace mantel in the drawing room? Position Andy Warhol's *Marilyn Monroe* silk screens in the dining room to watch over the antique, Chinese scholar's table? Or top an intricately carved, late nineteenth-century console with an ultra-contemporary painting? A good eye, of course, but sometimes it's simply because he can.

In line with the carefree lifestyle the designer savors here, which includes working on his novel and entertaining friends, there's neither too much nor too little in the way of furnishings. What *is* there, however, is signature Cohler: a mix of shapes, fabrics and textures, neutral tones punctuated with color, and always something to trigger curiosity. The man from up north has found his roots. "I'll be here 'til the wind blows me to Savannah," he says.

CHRISTOPHER COLEMAN

BROOKLYN, NEW YORK & ELIZAVILLE, NEW YORK

"I'm not a beige person," says Christopher Coleman, who never met a color he didn't like. He's also keen on unusual fabrics and proving good design can be achieved with any budget. The two homes he shares with his partner, couturier Angel Sanchez, exemplify these ideals well. Crayola brights explode against stark white in their New York apartment; woodsy tones capture the rural setting in the cabin upstate. Both are furnished primarily with inexpensive pieces found in off-beat places—with a few antiques thrown in for good measure—and altered in a profound way to align them with his design mantra: revise, recycle, redo.

"It's about using kindergarten colors in a mature manner."

When their Tribeca neighborhood became overcrowded with too many strollers and too many trendy coffee shops, Chris Coleman and Angel Sanchez decided it was time to cross the East River to Williamsburg, an arty, less gentrified community. A few days pounding the pavement and they found a duplex ten minutes from midtown Manhattan with an 18-foot-high, glass-walled living room and a terrace large enough for party overflow. The designer made only two major modifications: he reshaped the rectangular living room into an "L" and replaced the standard bedroom door with a red, patent-leather-wrapped sliding version.

The opposite of their previous apartment's black-and-white decorative scheme, Coleman explains he "wanted to push the color envelope and try things I don't do for clients." Sanchez agreed, and together they composed an exuberant palette of red, yellow, and blue, grounded with black and spiked with graphics. Always challenging himself, as much in his design work as with other aspects of life, Coleman painted the walls white, of which he says, "I'm accustomed to color, so these took some getting used to."

First came the kitchen. To tie it in with the rest of the apartment, he designed a vinyl wall covering in a bold, linear pattern for the far wall. Next was the floor, which Coleman carpeted because the original blond wood reminded him of a high school gym. Finally, "crunchy" parachute-cloth shades went up on the windows. As much fabric hound as furniture

aficionado, Coleman keeps his eyes open for the new and different. "Indoor-outdoor is this decade's Ultrasuede," he explains, "and the chenille on the sofa is a good example." He couldn't resist its luxurious texture and stainproof quality. Like the football-jersey cloth that covers the office chair, the upholstery of the two living room chairs is similarly unconventional. Coleman was in Avignon, France, when he spotted a sale sign in a store window. "Who could resist?" he laughs. "I went in and saw a $99, 4-by-6-foot Dhurrie rug with the kind of large-scale pattern I love, and that's impossible to find on fabric. I'm still amazed it ended up as upholstery for the chair by the window." Two years later, in Dubai, Coleman chanced upon the same retailer. No sale this time, but he found an angel-soft, wool blanket woven with an equally fabulous pattern. It now covers the other chair—both of them circa 1950s Czech, purchased a few years apart in Brooklyn.

Art is key to all Coleman interiors—the living room's ribbonlike metal sculpture created by Venezuelan Victor Valera comes from Sanchez's pied-à-terre in Caracas. If he can't find what he wants, however, he simply makes it. Behind the bed is a piece Coleman crafted by stretching a length of cotton over canvas, on either side of the bed are light fixtures he made of laminated silk placed over metal frames, and the large lacquered piece left of the ladder is the top of a table he once used in a designer showhouse.

ELIZAVILLE TWO IDEAS, TOGETHER

"Loons, beavers, the chorus of frogs. It's remote. You automatically turn off."

Exactly two hours and ten minutes up the Taconic State Parkway from Williamsburg is Elizaville, location of the couple's 1940s cabin. The former hunting lodge—complete with rifles hanging from the rafters and snowshoes on the walls—was in a sorry state when Coleman found it, but had a lot of perks as well: six acres of land, a wood-burning fireplace, and an absurdly low price. "I didn't care it was just 700 square feet," he recalls. "I knew I could transform it into a rustic yet luxurious home." Sanchez, however, whose style gravitates more toward clean lines and glass walls, had a difficult time envisioning the transformation. But as always when embarking on a joint venture, the two pooled their talents. Ultimately, they created a getaway where they can kick back, have a few guests, and enjoy leisurely meals whipped up by Coleman, who worked as a sous chef before turning to interior design.

Each sketched a layout of his vision—down to the position of the coffee table—and then came to terms by twining parts of both their concepts although Sanchez adds, "the cabin is 85 percent Chris." A mix of materials is important to the designer, apparent in the variety he chose that also complement the structure's era: vintage rattan chairs, Formica-topped, hairpin-legged table, and "cartoon-ish" shaped, chenille-upholstered Danish chair. The deerskin carpet, red "tree" lamp, and leather handles on the shoji-screen bedroom doors add an under-stated outdoorsy note. As for the wing chair on the porch purchased from an important auction house? "It was perfect," he says. "I simply removed the back's raised ornament, reupholstered it in Mongolian lamb, and turned the cabriole legs in for sleeker ones."

Stainless steel, they decided, would be efficient, and provide a slick counterpoint to the woodsy aura of the house. So again, drawing on Coleman's culinary past, the couturier and designer found the stove, refrigerator, range, even the industrial lighting in restaurant-supply shops on New York's Lower East Side. The final flourishes were to angle the porch screen outward for a more contemporary look, add a dramatic entry curtain, and build a slatted fence to create a living room–like feel for the spacious yard.

"In hindsight, we made some mistakes, like not putting in a dishwasher," confides Coleman, "but we're attached to it. The setting is wonderful and it has a good soul."

173

BENJAMIN NORIEGA-ORTIZ

NEW YORK, NEW YORK & SOUTH BEACH, FLORIDA

Benjamin Noriega-Ortiz believes in the "wow" factor. "Seeing a room for the first time should take your breath away," he says. His own homes, a New York City apartment and a house in South Beach, Florida, certainly do. Both are conceptually minimal, but with such flourishes as turkey feathers, floating fabrics, and shag carpeting, he gives new meaning to the word. The apartment is peaceful and enriched with curves in stark contrast to the clamor and hard edges outside the windows. The beach house sings with tropical colors and invites bare feet to tread on its cool, cement floors. The man who says he will never leave New York is comfortable in both.

"This is where I'll always live."

Noriega-Ortiz grew up in Puerto Rico and spent much of his time playing on the beach. Yet after one brief visit to Manhattan as a young adult, he knew it was the place to be. He's been there ever since. The two-bedroom-two-bath duplex he shares with life partner Steven Wine is in Chelsea, the epicenter of New York's contemporary art scene, and where he can be found almost every weekend visiting galleries. It's just the right size for the pair, especially with the 400-square-foot terrace they use to barbecue, decompress from work, and even sleep on occasionally. Two stuffed roosters—part of the designer's extensive "chicken art" collection—greet visitors on the stairs leading into the apartment, the country touch balanced by elegant aluminum-leafed walls.

Wine suggested the all-white scheme, something Noriega-Ortiz had never tried before. Done in ten variations of cream, fifty whites, and five different tones of silver for sparkle, the entire apartment brings to mind a puffy cumulus cloud. Keeping to the theme, he chose the furniture for its sculptured qualities, not its origin. "Value and history are invisible to the eye," he explains. Pieces are grouped according to use—conversation, dining, and working—and focus on gentle curves and touch-me textures: the Eames womb chair and ottoman date from the 1970s, the low, 1930s Kessler table is made of two separate pieces that fit together like a jigsaw puzzle, and an eighteenth-century-style chair made in 1940s Argentina was painted white by Noriega-Ortiz and

cushioned in Mongolian lamb's wool. The walls are finished with mica powder–infused Venetian plaster, their almost imperceptibly shimmery tint gradually changing as day turns to night.

Not ones for entertaining large crowds, partly due to the color scheme, Noriega-Ortiz smiles, saying that when they do, "Guests always have to take off their shoes, no excuses." Cooking for themselves, however, is a favorite pastime, and when it's too cold for the terrace, they take meals at the dining table that rests on a transparent, acrylic base, its top wrapped in faux leather as soft as a pair of kid gloves.

Soothing and tranquil, the master bedroom and sitting/guest room glow with ambient lighting, turkey- and coq-feathered lamps providing an instance of wit the designer adds to every residence. The only items not white here are the two bedside TVs—described laughingly by the designer as "a good way to keep peace." Nor is everything precious—the white chests are secondhand and the Ming tables are reproductions. Perhaps the pièce de résistance of the entire apartment, definitely of the master suite, is the enormous bathroom-spa—its bit of humor the Chinese bronze monkeys holding the soap. Designed to be open or closed off with simple white draperies, it is a serene place to begin and end the day.

"Houses tell stories," says Noriega-Ortiz, "through their color, shape, and texture." This one relates a tale of creativity and zest for life.

"I did the house like a small hotel. It's all about having fun."

Doing a great deal of work in Miami in the 1990s, Noriega-Ortiz decided to invest in a second home in South Beach. Within steps of the ocean, the 6,000-square-foot, Mediterranean-style stucco house was built in 1932, and contains five bedrooms plus a guest cottage. "A real party house," Noriega-Ortiz explains, "it was designed for non-stop entertaining." In step with Florida's bright colors, the ones he used were inspired by Fiestaware. But because they are used sparingly, he says, and the furniture is white or neutral in tone, "it looks more colorful than it really is."

Flying down every two weeks or so during the winter of its renovation Noriega-Ortiz was in vacation mode from the minute he stepped off the plane—hosting large get-togethers at the house, lolling on the beach, and rollerblading. "I basically lived in a tank top and shorts," he says, and the house reflects it. Sunny marigold reverberates downstairs. But it never overwhelms, due to the extensive use of white—ceiling beams, gossamer draperies cascading from the chair rail, an innovative take on wainscoting, denim upholstery, and a dominant faux marble fire-place. The lounge's dark wood frames and floor made of painted cement tiles similar to those popular in the 1930s ground the space and create a cool foil to the warm hues.

Diaphanous curtains set off the dining room, elegantly simple with the Eames chairs and a table made of a round slab of glass perched atop a tripod-shaped, aluminum base. "Every room should have something whimsical to cut the elegance," says Noriega-Ortiz. "The feather lamps do it in New York; here in the dining room, it's the pleated silk, overhead light fixture that Steven made. It resembles a giant garlic bulb, doesn't it?" The entire house draws from the natural beauty outside the front door: bedrooms are ocean blue, palm green, or hibiscus rose; crisp white woodwork, linens and window shades echo the clean, breezy atmosphere; glass vases hold fresh flowers; and austere, 1940s-era floor lamps catch the sun's rays.

Using the same guiding principle as with his home in New York—interiors as walk-in sculptures—Noriega-Ortiz proves the similarity of design and spoken language: One idea can be expressed in a multitude of ways, beautifully.

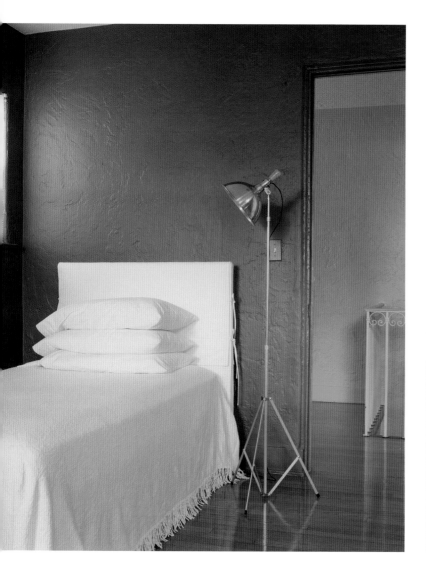

EVE ROBINSON

NEW YORK, NEW YORK & WATERMILL, NEW YORK

Eve Robinson's interiors defy typecasting. Cosmopolitan yet homey, simple yet complex, they wrap traditional backgrounds around modernist furnishings. The Manhattan apartment she shares with husband Joshua Wiener and their two sons is no exception. Exemplifying today's family-oriented lifestyle, it merges adult sophistication with comfort for their children: midcentury furnishings, adventuresome colors, and art. On weekends and holidays, the family decamps to a shingled, nineteenth-century house in historic Watermill, Long Island. The idea is similar, but more open and airy, with nature incorporated as a decorative element. One buttoned-up, the other carefree, both complement a life well-lived.

"We have rules, of course, but no area is off-limits to the kids."

It's an only-in-New-York kind of story," says Robinson. Newly married, she and Wiener were searching for a pre-war "classic six" on the Upper West Side. The apartment they found suited them well, but even so, the idea of adding on the one next door stayed top of mind. Eight years later the couple took action: "We asked the tenants, by now friends, if they would move if we found them a similar space," explains Robinson. "They said yes. We steered them to a wonderful new home. And everyone was happy."

Pulling the apartment together was a meeting of the minds between her and her husband, a contractor. "My husband is always full of good ideas," Robinson raves. "If I say no to three, he comes back with ten." One such collaboration began in the entrance foyer with a mosaic floor she designed but he installed. Explaining the tiny footprint on the center pattern, she says, "My oldest son was four when we were laying it, and he ran across the floor while the grout was still wet. We thought it was so sweet, we decided to leave it." The living room that follows picks up the pace. The furniture here represents Robinson's favorite eras—1930s and 1940s France, and 1950s Europe and the United States, for the most part—contemporary pieces are reserved for the bedrooms and family room. As she does for her clients, the designer found the majority of her furnishings from a well-honed network of local antique dealers, but the pair of chairs opposite the living room sofa claim a different provenance—Wiener found them discarded on the sidewalk in front of the building and later reupholstered them.

Robinson keeps the eye engaged with clever details that "reveal themselves over time," colors that cannot be boxed into one specific decade, and contrasting shapes. In the living room these include the leather English Arts & Crafts love seat surprisingly cushioned in a quilt reminiscent of classic Chanel handbags, the tones of the pillows and those in Robert Mangold's painting, and the round Biedermeier toiletry cabinet used as a side table. Entering the kitchen, she asks, "Don't the graphics remind you of the quilts from Gee's Bend?" They exemplify her skill in creating palettes to suit her personal taste. In the dining room she sets circles—the lacquered American Empire table and paper-shaded light fixture—against squares—the wallpapered ceiling and 1930s German, Macassar ebony chest. The drapes spark interest, too. Similar to those in the living room, but more formal, they are embellished by two bands of chocolate brown at the hem. This room is perfect for hosting adults-only dinner parties—that occur "not nearly often enough," Robinson says, laughing.

"It's a happy place where we enjoy the simple pleasures of life."

This place is scary!" shouted the boys, reacting to the depressing, dark walls in the eighth house they visited one day in 2003. But Robinson and Wiener weren't fazed: the possibilities were endless and they found the property's openness, hindered neither by too much privet nor too many trees, perfect. "A labor of love," the designer calls it. The first thing was to paint the walls white, leaving the original beams intact—ax marks are still visible on the biggest one that runs the length of the house—and later, enlarge windows, add a mud room, and finally, install solar panels.

Fabric selection is Robinson's primary method for determining color schemes and customarily her initial step. But this time she says, "I worked backwards," beginning with the living room carpet. "Maybe that's what made it more difficult than usual to find the upholstery for the 1950s chairs," she adds. Inspired by some pillows that came to her attention, she collaborated with the textile designer who had created them and developed a pattern and color palette unmistakably "Eve." Then, because weekends are for relaxing, not worrying, and it's inevitable people will come in wearing damp swimsuits with sand

on their feet, she had it printed on water- and soil-resistant linen. Also fuss-free are Paul Frankl's vintage, biomorphic-shaped painted-cork coffee table, and reclaimed-oak flooring, an ecologically responsible and durable choice.

Robinson had one more issue to resolve before calling the house complete, the master bedroom—so small, the only place to put the bed was in front of the window, not an option in her view. Her response? Panel it to match the walls and install two new windows on either side. The boys' only quandary was deciding which of their latest drawings should be framed and hung. When not playing football on the lawn or swimming in the pool, everyone loves gathering in the kitchen. The farmhouse table is "banged up, getting better with every ding," she says; 1950s and contemporary chairs are low-maintenance; and the bleached-coconut light fixture, reminiscent of a hula skirt, always makes her smile.

Robinson's revisionist indoor-outdoor theme is a "gentle balance between old and new." A few simple patterns, easy-on-the-eye color scheme, and uncomplicated shapes honor the house's classic exterior while infusing the interior with a fresh, modern look.

VICENTE WOLF

NEW YORK, NEW YORK & MONTAUK, NEW YORK

"Designing," explains Vicente Wolf, "is like writing a sentence. You need a clear idea of what you want to say, and then you must find the words to express it." His interiors crystallize his vision for a sense of design and architecture—not decoration—layered with pieces that, though very dissimilar, work together extremely well. Influenced by frequent trips to such countries as Borneo and Bhutan, both his New York City loft and getaway house on the eastern tip of Long Island are bathed in white and filled with art and antiquities. The similarities end there, however. The first is minimal, the second, cozily relaxed.

"The opposite of what's outside the windows—playful, sunny, dreamy."

was apprehensive when I moved to Hell's Kitchen in the late 1980s," Wolf remembers, "but I got used to it as I became accustomed to seeing the same cast of seedy characters hanging out on the street." Cleaned up since then, the neighborhood is convenient for him—a few yards from his office and showroom, and a short walk to the Broadway plays he frequently attends. While to Wolf it seems at times that it serves more as a way station than a home, it's a place that lifts his spirits even on the darkest days. "I jog around Central Park at dawn, go to the office, come back to go through my paces with the barbells and weight machine, then head off for the evening," he says.

He built the loft by combining a large photographer's studio with the apartment next door, gaining a sizable terrace in the process. As Wolf recalls, the studio was filthy when he got it—with a vile green floor and walls in terrible condition. But there were also immense windows framing the city below and all the sunlight he could want. Now, fully transformed, it measures a spacious 3,000 square feet, ideal for him and his housemate Nene the cat.

Wolf's first task was to knock down walls, rip out closets, and cloak everything in white. Then, as though blocking a stage set, he arranged the furniture into conversation areas behind a nineteenth-century teak screen, an airy room divider. Both are populated with pieces that travel through time and reach around the globe. The larger space is anchored by a Dutch Colonial daybed from Borneo, while the more intimate side poses a softly rounded sofa whose form echoes neoclassic settees with a nineteenth-century chair from Russia—updated with leather upholstery—and a 1960s acrylic chair.

Function, always an important consideration for Wolf, drives the design of the master suite: the bed's arched headboard backs up to a floating wall fitted with shelves on the reverse; not two, but three bedside tables hold his favorite white flowers and an ever-changing group of decorative objects; and in the bath, twenty-first-century lighting illuminates an antique Burmese table retrofitted with a stainless steel sink.

A renowned photographer in his own right and voracious collector, Wolf displays photography, sketches, and paintings by such past and present greats as Chuck Close, Damien Hirst, and Man Ray on wall rails and exquisite little chairs. "I like it when you can examine art closely," he says. Buddhas crop up everywhere, quite a few of them merely fragments. "It's that incompleteness I'm drawn to," he explains. "They heighten the sense I want here of an unfinished sketch."

"It's a grown-up home, a completed thought, moving seamlessly from the indoors out."

Wolf had just finished a client's house in Southampton, enjoying every minute he had spent on Long Island's eastern shores when a friend suggested nearby Montauk as a place Wolf might search for a weekend house of his own. He began looking seriously, but after five offers fell through, gave up. Then, out of the blue, his real estate agent called to say he had found perfection. Wolf disagreed: "It was so ugly!" The windows were undersized to say the least, the main entrance was via the basement, and there were no doors to access the side that fronted the ocean. But the location was unbeatable and he knew he could "make the house match the views."

He compares renovating the gray-shingled ranch to "taking a pretty girl with bad makeup and hair, wearing the wrong clothes, and styling her 'til she becomes a knock-out." He kept the footprint, but repositioned the entryway to overlook a landscaped terrain that slopes down to the beach and beyond to the ocean. Then he installed a new roof, put in floor-to-ceiling windows, redid the four bathrooms, and changed several rooms' original purposes. To achieve the "sybaritic ambience" he wanted, Wolf designed the antithesis of the loft. In the city, neutral-toned furniture is enveloped in bright white—a perpetually cheerful artificial sky. At the beach, where beautiful natural light abounds, he continues the theme of earth tones and whites, but grounds the interior with a flagstone floor and shifts the lightest colors to the slipcovers on the comfortable overstuffed sofas.

Wolf uses white abundantly—it's a good look for the casual furniture and keeps the focus on the panorama outside. Most of the seating is covered in low-maintenance cotton duck with a few flirtatious touches of voile, which, paired with Asian and African baskets, midcentury tables, and Eames chairs helps create a weekend mood. Scattered about are artifacts from his travels; even the porch hosts a Senufo chair from the Ivory Coast.

The house also has defined rooms, unlike the nearly doorless loft, making it better suited to visitors. When friends come Wolf wants them to feel coddled, with nothing to do but lie on the deck, swim, take a walk . . . even if he's working in the garden. Unlike most, he finds the often crowded, 100-mile drive from Manhattan calming. "You're always trying to be in control in the city. But the stop-and-go traffic on the highway is totally out of your control so there's nothing to do but sit and wait. Patience is something I learned in the East, where even the smallest transaction can take hours."

LEE BIERLY AND
CHRISTOPHER DRAKE

BOSTON, MASSACHUSETTS & PALM BEACH, FLORIDA

Lee Bierly and Christopher Drake personify the maxim, "Two heads are better than one." Business and life partners for more than thirty years, they have agreed to always try the other's design idea if one is "passionate about its workability." This, as they found in the course of designing their two homes, often turns out to be the best solution. The couple's Beacon Hill townhouse gives a nod to Boston's historically conservative designs, yet, thanks to their deft touch with antiques and gentle hues it is unassuming and easy-going. No surprise that in Palm Beach, where meetings can take place poolside, informality—albeit elegant—reigns. Neutrals and textures, a few hits of color, and what's outside the windows is brought in.

"Boston will always be home, no matter how far afield we may venture."

We never thought we'd live in a *house* here, or even a residence with multiple floors," says Lee Bierly. But when a broker showed him a 1910 townhouse on Charles River Square surrounded by flowering crabapple trees, he adds, "I knew Chris would love it." Diametrically opposite from their previous home—a contemporary, one-floor condominium—it is 21 feet wide with four floors and five fireplaces. The two faced extensive work prior to decorating, and as always, attacked the interior architecture, which they found "not quite Boston" and "lacking romance," first. Gutting the third floor, tagged for the master suite, revamping the kitchen, and laying maple flooring top to bottom were on the list. Finally they got to the décor. The men's aesthetic preferences differ: Drake likes color and is more traditional, influenced by European styles, while Bierly, a Californian who prefers neutrals, tends toward the contemporary. Borrowing from both perspectives, they found a common meeting point in a subtle garden theme: soft greens, yellows, and rose complemented by a sprinkling of outdoor statuary, patio chairs, a stone base for the dining table, and a smattering of small accessories like the porch lantern lighting the dining table. There are few patterns so

the "piles" of art and antiques, as Bierly modestly says, can take precedence.

Glancing about it is clear every piece was selected with scale, function, and comfort in mind, in addition to beauty. The imposing Portuguese desk and straw-backed Orkney chair are "strong enough to stand alone." An antique, gessoed French mirror hangs atop a mirrored wall in the living room doubling the sunshine and making it a favorite spot for Sunday mornings. A Gustavian desk was cut down to become the living room coffee table. "We don't buy just to buy," says Bierly, "and often sell one thing to make room for another." They like it when guests find an object interesting, picking it up for a closer look or to ask questions. "It's a great way to get a conversation going," they find. Among the collectibles that have stayed the course are nineteenth-century gilded clocks and artwork ranging from a Matisse drawing to a Mike and Doug Starn composite photograph from the 1980s.

The result is comfortable, elegant living: a place to relax together and host friends for sit-down dinners, suppers in front of the fire, and their annual holiday extravaganza. "We can't imagine ever leaving here," the two say.

"It's always fun on the island . . . like adult summer camp."

We feel like lost children sometimes—5,000 square feet is really too much," says Drake of their five-bedroom, five-bath Southern Colonial. But the extra rooms come in handy when the Boston staff, with whom they have worked for years, stays for local projects.

Bierly and Drake first laid eyes on the house in 2004, when it was, as Bierly remembers, "a damsel in distress," extensively damaged by Hurricanes Jeanne and Frances. And the previous owners' modifications? "All wrong," states Drake. But there were two architectural details that captured their interest: the stately, antebellum brick facade graced by an intricate iron balcony and the way room after room was saturated with sunlight. They felt sure an update that honored the house's original architectural integrity and personality was possible so they devoted two years to relocating baths and tearing down interior walls as well as demolishing, restoring, and repainting the outside. When the heavy lifting was finished, they focused on creating a look that fit the historic neighborhood, but would be sufficiently relaxed for their lifestyle.

Brilliant, lacquered marigold and garden statuary in the foyer set the cultivated yet casual tone for the rest of the house. There are fine furnishings everywhere—a Venetian tea table in the living room, marble-topped *bouillotte* table in the library and late-eighteenth-century *buffet à deux corps* displaying cream ware in the master bedroom. But there are also "primitive" textures to "take the curse off any formality," explains Bierly. Muslin cushions the antique French child's bed that their golden retriever sleeps on—at the foot of their own bed—burlap covers the walls of the sunroom, and the dining table's patchwork overskirt is pieced together from a variety of fabrics found in the firm's archive. The library's firewood bucket that sits beside the English desk is equally simple in its origins.

Be it walking on the beach, working in the office, or hosting fundraisers for the Historic Society of Palm Beach County and Palm Beach Preservation Foundation, "Living here is like being on a vacation," Drake says. "True," adds Bierly, "but then we wouldn't have our cell phones."

DESIGNER TIPS

RENEA ABBOTT

- Try hanging a wide mirror—that reaches all the way to the ceiling—above a sofa to give a room a focal point and make it feel larger.

- Add ribbon or tape that contrasts with a room's wallpaper along the baseboard, molding, or ceiling. It defines the space and ties in an accent color.

- Fire screens are back. Consider a simple model in tempered glass enhanced by understated metal detailing.

- Transform unattractive floors with sisal or sea-grass matting cut to size and bound in leather or tape. They work well with contemporary or traditional furniture.

- Personalize rooms with lampshades. Try a striped or plaid silk that coordinates with the upholstery fabric.

MARTHA ANGUS

- Dine by candlelight—it makes everyone relax and it's universally flattering!

- Use bold colors on the ceiling, walls, and even in the laundry room. Try hot pink in powder rooms and bright yellow in the coat closets.

- Perk up neutral walls, window coverings, and carpets with powerful art and accessories.

- Put indoor furniture out on the lawn to create an instant living room for big parties.

- Always hang pictures at eye level—finding the mean height for all adults in the house.

MICHAEL BERMAN

- Adding natural accents—driftwood, sea shells, a group of smooth monochromatic stones in a bowl—creates a sense of comfort in a room.

- Don't get hung up on trends and fancy labels. It's looks and function that count.

- Simplify. Too many estate sale finds give a room the appearance of a blown-up flea market.

- There is beauty in a mix—pair inexpensive and precious pieces.

- Go for big lighting—a glamorous and instant attention-grabber.

LEE BIERLY & CHRISTOPHER DRAKE

- Think of dark wood as an accent color. Four-poster beds, hardwood floors, and chair frames are beautiful paired with bright white and deep, leaf greens.

- Use floor coverings to quickly change a room's winter look to summer. Swap Orientals for sisal and broadloom carpets for a big cotton rug.

- Crisp, white organdy curtains are very today and simple to care for.

- Use the house's natural setting to inspire color schemes, furnishings, and even lighting.

- Decorating can be overwhelming, even to professionals. Relax and remember: Anything can be fixed.

LAWRENCE BOEDER

- Scan your space and ask yourself if each object is either useful or beautiful. If not, remove it.

- Trust your instincts. If you like it, it works.

- Make your house feel fresh by rearranging artwork and updating the lighting. These simple, inexpensive measures will make you appreciate what you already have.

- Proportion is key. A full-size rug makes a smaller room feel spacious; long drapes create the illusion of height.

- Spend a night in your guest room to find out if it has everything needed for a comfortable stay.

SUE BURGESS

- Devoting time to your home's design will satisfy on many levels—visual, tactile, and emotional.

- During the design process consider whether the style you have in mind will meet your functional needs.

- Keep things simple. Focus on a room's main elements first and allow accessories and art to evolve over time.

- Experiment with layouts using the furnishings you have on hand to help determine what works in a space.

- Think beyond what comes automatically.

BARCLAY BUTERA

- Buy with your heart.

- Think wallpaper for adding depth and texture to a room.

- Combine color, pattern, and texture in unexpected ways.

- Search out special pieces with stories behind them.

- Invest in items that transcend trend. You will keep timeless pieces forever.

ERIC COHLER

- Rules are meant to be broken.

- Don't be afraid of color.

- Use texture and geometry. Be bold.

- Think of the ceiling as the fifth wall.

- Edit, edit, edit!

CHRISTOPHER COLEMAN

- Even a small dose of color, when repeated a few times, is enough to keep the eyes dancing or unify an entire space.

- Explore wallpaper to add depth and interest. It's just as nice as Venetian plaster—and faster to apply.

- Give yourself and your guests a chuckle with a weird piece of art or an outlandish piece of furniture.

- Create a specific mood in each room with lighting. Try ambient, task, overhead, standing, sconces, and spots.

- Be flexible. Add wheels to furniture to make reconfiguring rooms easy for different purposes.

PAM DUNCAN

- Collect color swatches, magazine clippings, and pictures to inspire design plans.

- Take a cue from the environment. Use cool, breathable fabrics in hot climates, and warm, plush ones in cold.

- Think about details. Paint quality, cabinetry finishing, even curtain hems affect the overall look of a room.

- Don't clutter! Carefully selected and arranged accessories create the most impact.

- When in doubt, lay it out. Cut furniture patterns to scale from paper and arrange the pieces on a floor plan to find the best placement for each object.

ANDREW FISHER & JEFFRY WEISMAN

- Mix styles, periods, and materials for something unexpected and new.

- Add a bit of whimsy or fantasy to take the seriousness of each room down a notch.

- Consider comfort and function, but make sure the beauty of the interior is what stands out.

- Incorporate your personality into the décor—no one likes a room that feels anonymous or hotellike.

- Use color as a dramatic accent against strong, neutral backgrounds for a chic effect.

BEVERLY JACOMINI

- Symmetry creates harmony and a sense of well-being: try similar styles, equal numbers, coordinating fabrics.

- Remember, if it's not comfortable you won't use it. That means comfortable on the eyes, too!

- An interesting color in a room will be memorable and can define your personal style.

- Encourage children to start collections early. It makes accompanying you to auctions and flea markets more fun for them, and it can develop lifelong interests.

- Flowers and plants feed the soul. Incorporate them in simple ways by lining up small bud vases in the center of a dining table, or filling a large urn with leaves.

ALEX JORDAN

- Don't be afraid to invest in the architecture, materials, and finishes of a room. Everything will look better.

- Design your home for how you actually live, not how you think you should live.

- Be true to the architecture. Don't try to insert the interior of a saltbox cottage into an urban high-rise.

- Surprise yourself by stepping outside of your comfort zone. Try things you've never done or seen before.

- Bring fine art into your home. The Internet provides unparalleled access to excellent selections worldwide.

MOLLY LUETKEMEYER

- Paint is the easiest and least expensive way to experiment with color and can easily be changed.

- Avoid furniture sets. Explore and express your own style by mixing up eras, woods, and colors.

- Check out vintage stores the first time you happen across them. A quick look will decide if they're worth a return visit.

- Keep your eyes open. Inspiration for your next design project is all around—flower shops, clothing, movies.

- Incorporate awkward closet doors or beams into the architecture by painting or wallpapering them to match the wall.

JOHN PHIFER MARRS

- A window treatment should be more than just pretty. It should also offer privacy, light control, or insulation.

- Contrasts make a room unique—smooth with highly textured, elegant with humble, antique with contemporary, curvy with straight-edged.

- Mirrors are only as glamorous as what they reflect.

- Get the background right and the rest will be easy.

- Start with the bedroom. It's the first thing you see in the morning and the last you see at night.

BENJAMIN NORIEGA-ORTIZ

- Give every room a bit of the "wow" factor. A space should take your breath away.

- Color, shape, and texture affect the senses—use them to achieve a distinct mood.

- Repeat one color throughout a room to imbue it with a feeling of calm.

- Always select colors in which you look and feel good.

- Rooms flooded with natural light should have lighter color schemes than those that are not.

EVE ROBINSON

- Elevate kids' art to a higher level. Cover a family room wall with cork to create a pin-up board, or mat and frame their work before hanging.

- Less is more. Rooms feel calmer without clutter. Display as few items on surfaces as possible.

- Keep window treatments simple and in styles that let in the light.

- Try wallpapering the ceiling. It lifts eyes up and accentuates the height of a room.

- Good design rests in the details. Quality craftsmanship shows and will endure the test of time.

STEPHEN SHUBEL

- In a small living space, give the floors in every room the same treatment to create a sense of spaciousness. If hardwood floors are scuffed, simply paint them.

- Buy furnishings and accessories with some age to them for a boxy apartment; they provide character.

- Don't display all your tchotchkies and artwork at the same time. Change them with the seasons.

- Books and magazines add life to a room.

- Don't be too much of a neatnik or your home will lack soul and feel sterile.

VICENTE WOLF

- Ascertain each room's positives and negatives. When you design it, you will have a clear understanding about what to play up and what to hide.

- Clarify the direction to be taken—how the rooms will be used, styles, and colors—before beginning.

- Use the same color on walls and ceilings to make a room appear more spacious—unless it's very dark or very colorful. In that case, paint the ceiling white.

- Hang curtains and shades just below the ceiling to give the illusion of larger windows.

- Install kitchen and bathroom counters at 36 inches—the most practical height.

PHOTOGRAPHY CREDITS

Simona Aru and Luca Guarneri: 179 top, 179 bottom, 180, 181 bottom

Edmund Barr: 30 left, 30 right, 31

Gordon Beall: 139, 141, 142, 143, 144, 145, 147, 148, 149 left, 149 right

Antoine Bootz: 183, 184 left, 184 right, 185 top, 185 bottom

Robert Brantley: 219, 220 top, 220 bottom, 221

Fran Brennan: 109, 111, 112, 113 top 113 bottom, 115, 116 top, 116 bottom, 117

Julie Brothers: 45

Courtesy Barclay Butera, Inc.: 67

Jonn Coolidge: 47, 48, 49, 50, 51

Paul Costello: 189, 190, 191, 192, 193

Grey Crawford: 21, 22, 23, 24, 25, 27, 28, 29 left, 29 right, 53, 54, 55 top, 55 bottom, 57, 59, 60, 61 top, 61 bottom, 63, 64 top, 64 bottom, 65

© Paul Doughty: 119

David Glomb: 135, 136 left, 136 right, 137

Philip Harvey: 35, 36 top, 36 bottom, 37, 38 left, 38 right, 39

Ken Hayden: 177, 178

Stephen Karlisch: 87, 89, 90, 91 left, 91 right, 92, 93

David Duncan Livingston: 19

Mark Lohman: 69, 70, 71 top, 71 bottom, 74, 75 top, 75 bottom

Peter Margonelli: 187, 195, 196 top, 196 bottom, 197

Peter Medilek: 7, 9, 10 left, 10 right, 11

Dana Meilijson: 165, 167, 168, 169 top, 169 bottom, 171, 172, 173 left, 173 right

Courtesy Meredith Corporation. Photography by Gordon Beall: 211, 213, 214 top, 214 bottom, 215, 216, 217

Bärbel Miebach: 181 top

Matthew Millman: 13, 14 left, 14 right, 15, 16 top, 16 bottom, 17

Nancy Nolan: 95, 96 top, 96 bottom, 97

Grant Perigo: 199

Dan Piassick: 105, 106, 107 top, 107 bottom

Kate Russell: 77, 79, 80, 81 top, 81 bottom, 83, 84, 85 left, 85 right

© Karen Sachar: 99

Thomas Hart Shelby: 175

Tony Soluri: 121, 122 top, 122 bottom, 123, 125, 126 top, 126 bottom, 127

Tony Soluri/Architectural Digest, © Condé Nast Publications: 129, 131, 132, 133 top left, 133 top right, 133 bottom left, 133 bottom right

Frances Smith: 151

Alexander Steinhaus: 33

Courtesy Veranda magazine. Photography by Jeff McNamara: 159, 160, 161, 162, 163

Courtesy Veranda magazine. Photography by Casey and Anne Sills: 101, 102, 103 left, 103 right

Courtesy Veranda magazine. Photography by Vicente Wolf: 201, 202 top, 202 bottom, 203, 204–5

William Waldron, courtesy Eric Cohler Design: 53, 54, 55, 56, 57 left, 57 right

Vicente Wolf: 207, 208 top, 208 bottom, 209

Dominique Vorillon, courtesy House Beautiful: 41, 42, 43 top left, 43 top right, 43 bottom left, 43 bottom right

Scot Zimmerman: 73